T0116467

Cambridge Elements ☰

Elements in Publishing and Book Culture
edited by
Samantha Rayner
University College London
Rebecca Lyons
University of Bristol

YOUNG PEOPLE, COMICS, AND READING

Exploring a Complex Reading Experience

Lucia Cedeira Serantes
Queens College, City University of New York

CAMBRIDGE
UNIVERSITY PRESS

CAMBRIDGE
UNIVERSITY PRESS

University Printing House, Cambridge CB2 8BS, United Kingdom

One Liberty Plaza, 20th Floor, New York, NY 10006, USA

477 Williamstown Road, Port Melbourne, VIC 3207, Australia

314–321, 3rd Floor, Plot 3, Splendor Forum, Jasola District Centre, New Delhi – 110025, India

79 Anson Road, #06–04/06, Singapore 079906

Cambridge University Press is part of the University of Cambridge.

It furthers the University's mission by disseminating knowledge in the pursuit of education, learning, and research at the highest international levels of excellence.

www.cambridge.org
Information on this title: www.cambridge.org/9781108445344
DOI: 10.1017/9781108568845

First published 2019

A catalogue record for this publication is available from the British Library.

ISBN 978-1-108-44534-4 Paperback
ISSN 2514-8524 (online)
ISSN 2514-8516 (print)

Cambridge Elements

Young People, Comics, and Reading

Exploring a Complex Reading Experience

Elements in Publishing and Book Culture

DOI: 10.1017/9781108568845
First published online: February 2019

Lucia Cedeira Serantes
Queens College, City University of New York

Author for correspondence: Lucia Cedeira Serantes,
lucia.cedeiraserantes@qc.cuny.edu

ABSTRACT: Scholars and professionals interested in the study of and engagement with young people will find this Element relevant to deepening their understanding of young people's reading practices with comics and graphic novels. Comics reading has been an understudied experience despite its potential to enrich our exploration of reading in our currently saturated media landscape. This study is based on seventeen in-depth interviews with teens and young adults who describe themselves as readers of comics for pleasure. These interviews provide insights about how comics reading evolves with readers and what readers consider a good or bad reading experience. Special attention is paid to the place of female readers in the comics community and to the material aspects of reading. From these readers, one begins to understand why comics reading is something that young people do not "grow out of" but is an experience that they "grow with."

KEYWORDS: reading and readers, comics and graphic novels, teenagers, young adults

ISBNs: 9781108445344 (PB), 9781108568845 (OC)
ISSNs: 2514-8524 (online), 2514-8516 (print)

Contents

1 Situating This Study: Young People's Reading Practices and Comics As a Reading Choice

Historically, comics have been denigrated as a reading choice and with them, their readers and their readers' experiences.[1] This situation is slowly changing for comics: media are paying attention to new releases and adaptations; libraries are including comics in their collections and doing programming around them, especially dedicated to youth; scholars are studying comics and their creators; and educators are finding ways to integrate comics into classrooms. However, little is known about comics' readers, something this Element tackles. With readers at the center of this Element and seeking to intersect two different fields of study, I have a twofold objective:

1. In relation to the study of the reading experience, I am looking to show how comics readers, especially young people, are valuable contributors to our understanding of contemporary reading; moreover, I believe the study of comics reading provides invaluable insights about how reading fits into the busy lives of young people.

---

[1] I touch briefly on this status in Section 1.2, but if the reader would like to expand on this aspect of comics and reading, the following texts support this exploration: Gabilliet (2010) and Wright (2003) contextualize comics among historical, social, and cultural developments in the United States, and Lent (1999) focuses on international anti-comics campaigns; Nyberg (2016, 1998) examines in depth the Comics Code and the relationship between adult gatekeepers and children's comics reading (2002); Tilley (2012) debunks Fredric Wertham's research project that guided many of the attacks on comics reading during the 1950s; Cedeira Serantes (2013) connects librarians' past attitudes regarding comics and comics reading with present stereotypes.

2. In relation to the study of comics, I am seeking to open up the discussion about comics reading beyond the experience of the fan and to explore the role of comics as reading materials for young people.[2]

The literature review that follows is not meant to be comprehensive but targeted, pointing to the studies and scholars that are in direct conversation with this study and that also situate its origins and boundaries. Before starting, a note about terminology is also needed. The term *comics* is used as an umbrella term to bring together the many material formats that the medium assumes. Although I chose primarily to use *comics*, the terms *comic books* and *graphic novels* might also be used because they are heavily represented in the discourse of specific fields and research projects, such as media studies and library professional literature. For discussions focused on the medium and its terminology, the reader can start with Scott McCloud's classic text *Understanding Comics* and then move to other scholarly discussions (e.g., Sousanis, 2015; Stein & Thon, 2013; Hatfield & Svonkin, 2012; Goldsmith, 2010; Heer & Worcester, 2009; Chute & DeKoven, 2006).

Finally, to avoid disappointing some readers, in this Element, one is not going to find results of large reading surveys or closed readings of any particular titles or genres. As I expand on in Section 1.3 dedicated to methodology, this is a qualitative study focused on the experiences of a group of readers who care for and enjoy different types of comics. They speak about how they became interested in this medium, how comics reading fits into their

---

[2] The concept of reading material extends from library and information science and education, both in their scholarly discipline and in their professional practice. *Reading material* is used as an encompassing term to refer to any type of document (books, magazines, newspapers, websites, etc.) that could be read by library patrons or students. To avoid confusion, I use the term *materiality* to discuss aspects related to physical and digital attributes of comics.

lives, what they like in comics, and what they look for in a comics reading experience. With these themes as guidance in our interviews, other more specific and unintended topics emerged, such as comics and their materiality and the importance of gender issues for female readers. To know more about the participants before starting reading, you may move on to the methodology section.

1.1 Readers and the Reading Experience: Bringing Comics Readers into the Discussion

This Element sees itself as part of a larger body of scholarly literature that focuses on looking at reading, mainly reading for pleasure, with the reader and the reading experience at the center. Reading is not a one-dimensional or disconnected practice and there are many ways of reading and many materials to read, a point that has provoked recent calls for a multidimensional approach to the study of reading (Arizpe & Cliff Hodges, 2018; Cliff Hodges, 2016; Mangen & van der Weel, 2016) and the reading experience (Rothbauer, Skjerdingstad, McKechnie, & Oterholm, 2016). One of the characteristics of this reader-centered research is that it reveals the complexity, situatedness, and multilayered nature of the reading experience, something that I am not the first one to note (i.e., Fuller & Rehberg Sedo, 2013; Howard, 2011, 2009; Mackey, 2011; Rothbauer, 2011, 2004; Collinson, 2009).

Some of the aforementioned studies are focused on young people, and in the following I lay out an intellectual path of sorts that this Element shares with some of these studies. The scholarly research of Paulette Rothbauer provided much guidance, inspiration, and motivation for this project (2011, 2009, 2004). She studied the reading experience and being a reader as an identity in the lives of queer young women and young people in rural environments. For instance, from her work on a Canadian rural municipality four spatial factors emerged that influenced the reading lives of young people: the physical availability of reading selections and its positive/ negative impact on the reading lives of young people, the public library as a place of childhood reading and as a place evaluated by what it does not offer, the default place of the Internet as a site to make and enact reading choices, and the lack of time and space for reading (2009). An outcome of the combination of these factors is the idea of the nonactive teen reader: "the limited reading choices found throughout the municipality combined with few opportunities to enact a reading identity make the concept of the teen reader unviable" (p. 479). Her conclusions highlighted the situatedness of the reading experience, making the context of reading (spaces, temporal structures, institutions, etc.) indispensable to consider when one is exploring the reading experience. Equally inspiring was her work with seventeen young queer, lesbian, and bisexual women, which challenged some commonplaces related to the reading experience. The voices of these readers situated Rothbauer in a privileged position to question commonplaces in regards to the functions of reading. For instance, the metaphor of reading as escape did not adequately describe some of the roles that reading played in their lives (2004, pp. 55–56), since some participants seemed to read "less for *escape from* than for *engagement with* the worlds in which they live" (p. 65). Another of Rothbauer's themes explored the use of reading as a way to increase social participation in larger communities, a theme that connects strongly with her overall idea of reading for possibilities. As she explains it:

> Reading for possibilities gives them a coherent and perhaps, cohesive, sense of self. Reading for community represents their desire to move this "self" into a larger social arena to make connections with other lesbian, bisexual and queer women. (p. 111)

As I discuss later, my participants practice reading both as something social and as something solitary, depending on what role comics reading is playing in their lives at a precise moment. In the end, both Rothbauer and I are finding ties between the reading experience and the lives of our participants, trying to interrogate, explore, and challenge common understandings about an often neglected population (young adult readers) and, in my case, an undervalued practice (reading comics).

Rothbauer has also worked with McKechnie and Ross (Ross, McKechnie, & Rothbauer, 2018, 2006) in a project that sought to provide scholarly support for the work of librarians and educators in explaining why reading for pleasure is "a Good Thing" (Ross et al., 2018, p. vii). One of the first issues that Rothbauer tackles about young people's reading is the "do they read or not" question (pp. 104–109). This debate is a common starting point in conversations about teen reading; its importance rests on its direct connection with definitions of what reading is and what is considered acceptable reading. Comics, as well as series books or genre reading, have been central in these discussions. Elsewhere I have explored in depth the narratives that librarians construct around comics readers (Cedeira Serantes, 2013) that have historically also been strongly tied to the discussions about "what is acceptable to read." It is important, then, to briefly note the stereotypes that surround comics reading and young people. As I noted at the beginning, comics (under the label of *graphic novels*) are increasingly characterized as rich, complex, challenging, diverse, and multilayered reading material, but it is commonplace to introduce teen readers of comics as misfits, loners, reluctant readers, and patrons who lack reading skills or discriminating tastes. The richness of the material should imply a similar richness in comics' readers (Cedeira Serantes, 2013, pp. 130–131). Based on the complexity of the reading material, teen readers could be portrayed or studied as savvy, complex, experimental, multimedia readers.

A reading material that has experienced a similar path to comics is series books. Both were attacked in comparable ways by cultural gatekeepers accusing them of physically and intellectually harming innocent youth; both were not considered real reading and they were missing from educational and cultural institutions. In the midst of the success of the criticized *Goosebumps* (R. L. Stine) series, Ross published an article defending the role of series books in the life of adult avid readers (1995). The originality and strength of her research comes from the voices of the readers who helped her discover the supporting and entertaining role that series books had for them. Ross pointed to the importance of familiarizing oneself with the conventions of reading, acquiring a "literary competence" (p. 228). Series books support the development of this familiarity because of some of the characteristics they are criticized for, such as their formulaic plots and structures as well as their stereotyped characters. These elements provide a familiar and safe reading experience, one that is easy to engage with and enjoy. If we conceptualize reading and/or being a reader as a practice that accompanies readers, especially young readers, in their life development, any kind of reading should be considered valuable because it helps the reader to develop or cement literacy (and literary) skills as well as it provides early exposure to and awareness of contextual aspects of reading such as varied reading formats or the difference between assigned and pleasure reading.

Building on Ross's research, Howard (2011) confirmed that young readers often choose "a book for pleasure and then find in it insights related to themselves, their lives, and their problems" (p. 53). Howard carried on a series of focus group discussions with a total of sixty-eight twelve- to fifteen-year-olds at junior high schools to explore the role of pleasure reading in their lives, concluding that pleasure reading brings three broad benefits: it enhances academic performance, social engagement, and personal development (pp. 47–48). As I discuss later, comics can also function as channels for social engagement, and they are definitely entangled in the personal development of some of my participants.

Margaret Mackey is another important researcher to bring to the conversation. Although her work connects more strongly with the study of literacies, the curiosity about the rich media ecology young people live in makes it central for any contemporary discussions of young people's reading. Mackey makes young people's participation central to her research projects but does not focus on a specific age range or reading/viewing format (2011, 2007a, 2007b), making her work perfect to highlight the differences, interrelations, and commonalities among a rich variety of texts and formats (novels, short stories, e-books, graphic novels, videogames, movies, or poems) and also among rich groups of participants: elementary and junior high students (2007a), under-graduate students (2011), and adults and young adults (2007b). In *Literacies across Media* (2007a), Mackey concentrates on the experiences of a group of students with a variety of texts: picture books, novels, movies, computer games, and e-books, including some titles in more than one format. Note that, even though Mackey chose a variety of texts, comics are not represented in her selection. However, the two students who are the focus of her analysis in two chapters briefly mention reading comics as part of their media consumption (pp. 35, 48). Evidently Mackey could not feasibly study every media text available in contemporary culture. In contrast, she offered comics in her research project with older readers (2007b), and I focus on her treatment of the topic later. The concepts of personal salience and fluency of access revealed themselves as basic in the process of selection among texts, especially in a saturated media landscape (2007a, pp. 88–92). Participants judged each text according to its own characteristics and merits and they decided which materials to read based on interest (salience) or familiarity with the medium (fluency). These two ideas are relevant when one thinks about comics. They mix text and image, something that we are familiar with as children because of picture books, but that many young adults, and especially adults, leave behind or are encouraged to leave behind after childhood. Reading comics activates a series of different skills than reading plain text does, so fluency of access is an idea to consider when interviewing readers. The diversity of styles and conventions, among titles not just from different countries but also from different genres, confirms the importance of the idea of fluency. Another relevant idea is that of the physicality of reading. Mackey dedicated a chapter to the physical differences between reading print and digital texts, and, more precisely, the role of hands. Comics are published in variety of formats. If one visits a comics store, he or she can encounter, for example, a thirty-two-page softcover comic book, a trade paperback that collects several comic books, the standard format of a European album, and a hardcover graphic novel in landscape format as thick as 300 pages long. With the advent of digital platforms like Comixology or Izneo, digital reading needs to be added to this list of physical formats. Evidently the experience of reading any of these materials is different, both intellectually and physically.

In *Mapping Recreational Literacies*, Mackey decided to investigate adults and young adults because "[t]he concept of fully literate adulthood occupies a strange default position of invisibility – the end-point and measure of literacy education but taken for granted, under-explored, and under-described" (2007b, p. 3). Mackey recruited nine participants from nineteen to thirty-six years of age and looked at how they engage in different literate activities in their leisure time, meeting with each of them separately and finishing with ten hours of taped and transcribed sessions for each participant. Mackey included graphic novels in this work and dedicated a section to the possible challenges and peculiarities of the comics medium (pp. 108–111). She defined graphic novels as follows: "a graphic novel is something like a grown-up comic, a larger incarnation of a popular method of telling stories through words and images" (p. 108). Mackey detected a strong link between some of the abilities needed to read graphic novels and hypertext and digital games (p. 110). Her concluding sentences for that brief analysis of the medium, although focused on the text, are highly stimulating. She noted that "young readers are learning how to manage sophisticated forms of data-handling and interpretation from sources that have regularly been perceived as humble at best, pernicious at worst" (p. 111). If we shift the thought, can we say that the readers of these texts are also sophisticated readers? I believe Mackey certainly helps to probe this point from a literacies-based perspective, and the work that scholars from education have done to connect comics and multimodal literacies exemplifies this point (e.g., Jacobs, 2013; Hammond, 2012). To conclude the analysis, Mackey speculated that maybe her participants have an attitude toward the medium that supports the idea that "a good enough reading" is plenty for this format (p. 148) or that with the diversity of formats in current media ecology, "finding the point of good-enough is actually a reasonable survival strategy" (p. 148).

Mackey's latest work on young adult reading, *Narrative Pleasures in Young Adult Novels, Films, and Video Games* (2011), focuses on narrative comprehension: "I want to explore some story-processing skills and strategies that generate fictional understanding in three specific media: book, game, [and] film" (p. 3). The group of participants comprised twelve young people from nineteen to twenty-two years of age, nine male and three female, who met in groups of three to read a novel, *Monster* by Walter Dean Myers, to watch a film, *Run Lola Run*, and to play a digital game on PlayStation 2, *Shadow of the Colossus*, always from beginning to end. Mackey describes the readers as ordinary. She also addresses the male predominance in the sample, explaining that it is recurrent in samples requiring game experience and that her priority is "to gain insight into narrative thinking that included the element of game experience" (p. 35). Even though this Element focuses on comics, discussions about movies, television shows, and other reading materials were unavoidable during the interviews, sometimes because I asked questions about them, at other times because my participants referred to them for comparison. Mackey reaches a similar conclusion about her participants: "[t]he first fact about the young people in this project is that they cannot address any explicit question about a single medium or format, no matter how monomodally phrased or intended, from any standpoint but that of multimodal interpreter. However singular the focus, their stance is unavoidably comparative" (p. 200). In connection with the idea of media diversity, Mackey defends movements of expansion and inclusion in relation to the educational canon in order to support the potential skills youth develop in their everyday lives. Reading is an elusive process. Mackey describes it as unique, personal, and distinctive and points to the fact that "the experience inside the black box of each interpreter's mind was specific to each of them and was *felt* and *thought* in different ways" (p. 201). This is why the more information, from varied perspectives, that we can accumulate about this intimate and particular process, the better we will be able to understand the potential needs of youth as readers, students, library patrons, and, ultimately, as citizens.

Mackey's research shows how slowly comics were being considered as necessary when one had to represent the richness of the current media landscape. However, perhaps not surprising, there are not many scholarly intersections between the topics of reading for pleasure and comics reading, despite the fact that young adult and adult readers have been consistently reading comics as a leisurely activity since the early twentieth century (Gibson, 2015; Wright, 2003). Education and library and information studies are the scholarly fields where more studies emerge, but, due to the professional focus of both fields, most of the research has concentrated on denying or justifying the presence, use, and value of comics in classrooms or libraries. In 1944, Josette Frank highlighted the appeal of comics to "children of all ages, of high and low I.Q., girls as well as boys, good readers and nonreaders, in good homes and poor ones – they *all* read the comics, and read them with an avidity and an absorption that passes understanding" (1944, p. 214). Frank was one of few vocal defenders of comics during the 1940s and 1950s; recognizing and highlighting this broad and diverse audience was (and still is) a rarity. Carol Tilley's historical research offers a comprehensive portrait of the opinions and responses of youth librarians and some educators to the increasingly popular comic books (2007). Tilley has also debunked some of the research by Fredric Wertham that helped to sustain those negative opinions and attacks (2012).

Focusing on contemporary reading and comics, Clare Snowball has addressed the lack of information about teen readers of graphic novels in her doctoral dissertation, Graphic Novels: Enticing Teenagers into the Library (2011), and three previous articles that advanced her doctoral work (2008, 2007, 2005). Her dissertation focused on the connection between graphic novels and reluctant teenage readers and the role that those materials assumed in these readers' reading and library participation. Her research sample comprised forty teenagers, averaging fourteen years of age, from metropolitan Perth (Australia) high schools. The participants share diverse attitudes toward reading that Snowball divides into five types: avid, dormant, intermediate, ambivalent, and those who find reading irrelevant (2011, p. 166). The fact that the participants were not just comics readers provides invaluable information about generalizations in the literature about teenagers overwhelmingly liking comics.

One common belief that was quickly challenged in Snowball's research was teen familiarity with graphic novels (2011, p. 171). Most of Snowball's participants had heard about graphic novels, but their attempts to define them were intriguing: Kylie said, "I think these are picture books"; Anna openly questioned, "Isn't it [graphic novels] just like comics?"; and Cassie said, "I always thought comics were like a small magazine, not a book" (p. 77).

Even this small sample already illustrates the diversity of teens' attitudes toward and relationships with reading and comics reading. Snowball notes that many students who disliked graphic novels had not experienced them before (p. 81). The reasons for their dislike varied; some of them simply did not like them. Others were very critical of the visual aspect of comics; for example, Ellen claimed to hate pictures and linked them to children's books (p. 89); David, an avid reader, felt graphic novels were "too short, too simple" and "no better than picture books," and he thought that conventional books were "better" (pp. 81–82). Three participants pointed out the difficulty of reading and following speech bubbles (p. 81), and many readers expressed difficulties when reading traditional manga published right to left. Most participants also shared a lack of awareness about the presence of graphic novels in their school libraries' collections, even the participants who declared themselves to be comics readers. Therefore, the presence of graphic novels could not be equated to knowledge of or interest in the medium (p. 197). These materials were sometimes shelved with the picture books, possibly adding to the students' confusion. The quality of the collections is not examined, but one participant, Ryan, described the graphic novels in his library as "all the crappy ones" (p. 77).

A welcomed change in the perspective taken toward comics and readership can be seen in the recent edition of Goldsmith's professional book about comics and readers' advisory (2017). Instead of focusing just on text recommendations, Goldsmith dedicates a majority of chapters to provide advice and to study issues related to different types of readers: by age (children, teens, and adults) and by expertise (experienced or traditional readers, emerging readers, and developing readers) and how to approach those readers with comics titles. This strategy makes visible for librarians the potential plethora of readers who can be interested in comics reading and how complex it can be to collect and recommend comics that represent and serve that richness.

The work about comics and literacies in the field of education cannot be omitted in a discussion about reading and comics. The status of comics in education has evolved rather quickly in recent years. This should not be surprising since historically the discipline has been more welcoming of comics, at least trying to figure out how to utilize the obvious attraction this medium had for young people. For instance, Harvey Zorbaugh wrote in his editorial in an issue of the *Journal of Educational Sociology* dedicated to comics:

> Somewhere between vituperation and complacency must be found a road to the understanding and use of this great medium of communication and social influence. For the comics are here to stay. (1944, p. 194)

However, librarianship, societal attacks, and their resulting censorship during the 1950s also affected the interest and output of education researchers. In 2011, Sabeti introduced her reader-centered article about a group of teen readers in a graphic novels reading group at a Scottish high school with the following description of the relationship between comics and education: "Comics and education is usually synonymous with low literacy level, reluctant readers and a predominantly male audience" (2011, p. 137). Comparatively, a positive advance can be noted in 2017, when Botzakis, Savitz, and Low concluded their literature review on adolescent literacies, graphic novels, and comics with the following thought:

> Taking up these texts offers opportunities for all types of adolescents, those who are skilled and those who struggle. What is more, because of the increasingly diverse set of creators, characters, and situations being represented in comics (Royal, 2012), many formerly underrepresented groups can

now find familiar faces and read about [them] in the pages of comics. (2017, p. 319)

During the early 2010s, both Botzakis (2011a, 2011b, 2009) and Sabeti (2013, 2012a, 2011) published some of the more innovative reader-centered research in education, advocating for a deeper understanding of "what people do with texts" before using them in the classroom and thus connecting comics reading to issues of identity construction, social contexts of reading, and literacies, broadly understood. To conclude this section, I bring back a quote from Ross's article about series books: "[i]f we want to make sense of these reading preferences, we have to let the readers speak in their own voices" (1995, p. 215). I believe that if we want to both expand and deepen our scholarly knowledge about the contemporary reading experience, we need to talk to young readers (in this case, comics readers) and to explore the contexts where their experience occurs and how it fits into their overall cultural habits.

1.2 Media and Communication Studies: Finding Readers among the Comics Community

The interest of media and communication studies in comics reading can be traced back to the rise of comic books during the 1930s and 1940s and the subsequent backlash during the 1950s. During the mid-1930s, the popularity of comics among children became a reality when stapled collections of newspaper comics were first used as an advertisement gift and later published on their own, aimed at a young audience (Gabilliet, 2010, pp. 194–196). In April 1938, the first Superman story was published as part of the *Action Comics* anthology. Reprints of newspaper comics were not enough to keep up with the demand, and original stories started to populate new comic books. It is especially important to note that children would acquire them independently and share them among themselves, avoiding traditional cultural gatekeepers such as parents, teachers, and librarians. Comic books also became popular among adults, especially among soldiers during the Second World War, but their main audience was youth, as different surveys from the time noted (Gabilliet, 2010, p. 198). This popularity and the expansion of the publishing market to storylines deemed more controversial by adults provoked a backlash in the 1950s. Nyberg summarizes the criticisms against comics and comics reading in three types that happened simultaneously:

- "criticism of comics' detrimental effect on children's reading;
- criticism of comic book content's failure to uphold the moral values of society; and
- criticism of the behavioral effects of comic book content, which desensitized children to violence and promoted juvenile delinquency" (2016, p. 25).

A consequence of this backlash would be the establishment of the Comics Code in 1954, but the popularity of comics among children also sparked interest from scholars, as I briefly noted before, from education, for example, but also from media and communication. It is not a coincidence that this discipline equates the experience of reading comics with the experience of fandom, especially if comics fandom is understood as a young, male audience who, for the most part, consume mainstream superhero texts. In 1948, Wolfe and Fiske reported on one of the first major studies about comics reading in their article "The Children Talk about Comics." Although groundbreaking and progressive for its time, it also starts a path that associates comics reading with the experience of becoming or being a fan.

Wolfe and Fiske's study identifies three types of comic readers: comic book fans, moderate readers, and indifferent or hostile readers; however, the report largely focuses on the first type of readers, the fans, "whose interest in comics is patently violent and excessive" to the point of potentially neglecting any other activity (Wolfe & Fiske, 1949, p. 22). The study clearly highlights the "problems" of "excessive" comics reading, but its general conclusions about comics reading are, at least, ambiguous. At the same time that it points to many of the traits of a stereotypical modern fan, it also moderately defends reading comics. It studies comics as material to be left behind by mature readers who use nonfiction comics "as a tool for the real adventure which is life itself" (p. 34). It concludes that most of the behavioral issues presented by fans were not caused by comics but existed beforehand. Two characteristics make Wolfe and Fiske's work rather unique, even by present-day standards. First, their study recognizes the existence of differences in the experience of comics reading; although certainly focusing on the fan, it shows interest as well in the moderate reader. Second, Wolfe and Fiske grant value in reading comics in that these materials are seen as any other reading material for children, although material that children eventually grow out of. This idea that a good child reader will grow out of comics reading is still prevalent, as I noted in some of the conversations with my participants.

The prominence of fan studies as a site of knowledge about the relationship among readers, fans, and comics has resulted in an imbalance in the description not only of the experience but also of the readers themselves. Some scholars have already noted this. In his study of American comics, French scholar Gabilliet (2010) dedicates a section to fans, looking at the phenomenon from a historical point of view. Nevertheless, he also notes two other types of readers: readers and letter writers. Despite this focus on the fan, Gabilliet notes that "[t]he actual readership is an informal community in which a silent majority coexists with a vocal minority, whose ideas and preferences are not necessarily in line with those of the majority of the purchasers of a given title" (p. 257). Gabilliet blames this silence and lack of "cultural activism" on the inability to "construct a reliable representation of occasional or non-passionate readers" (p. 257). Previously, in his research project focused on comics publisher Milestone Media, Brown (2001) examined how readers used Milestone's comics to construct and understand race and gender. At some point, Brown contends that 10 to 20 percent of the comic book audience are fans but also recognizes the difficulty of distinguishing between an occasional reader and a fan (p. 61). Parsons (1991), in his widely cited study of the audience for superhero comics, notes the metamorphosis in comic book readership in terms of both age and cultural sophistication. Parsons focuses on the audience of comic books published by Marvel and DC, again breaking it into three groups (p. 81):

- Fan collectors: they are the oldest, with a higher income and level of education.
- Older non-collectors: these readers are attracted to independent titles, with realistic themes.
- The bulk of the readership: fifteen- to twenty-year-old males largely involved with superhero and fantasy comics.

Pustz's work (1999) describes how comics culture arises from a community that, although diverse, finds appreciation for the comics medium to be the unifying element (p. 204). In his work, the main site of analysis is a comics store and its employees and customers are the main sources for his research data. Pustz considers fan involvement as a major factor in defining comics culture. The practices that define this involvement do not separate between readers and fans. For example, in the first pages of the chapter dedicated to study of "the spectrum of contemporary readers" (pp. 66–109), Pustz notes that some comics readers "fit the traditional idea of fans" and others are described as "fanboys," while a third group does not want to be related to mainstream comics and "identif[ies] [itself] as fans for alternative comics" (p. 67). Pustz recognizes the existence of "regular readers" who are not as involved with fan activities, but his emphasis falls on the fact that they "remain devoted to and identify with comic books" (p. 68).

In a study influenced by Pustz's work, Woo (2011) attempts to expand the theorizing of comics shops, especially as sites to extend the understanding of comics reception and further comics studies beyond the reader–text relationship. The importance of the study is undeniable, especially the author's effort at theorizing the many roles that comics stores can play in the experience of a comics reader. In his conclusion, Woo notes that readers and collectors clearly produce different spaces and their reception should not be assumed a priori. In order to investigate these differences, he points to an issue highly relevant for the purposes of my study:

> We ought to replace the ideal reader posited by abstract theories of reception or naïvely presupposed by scholarly "reading" of cultural texts with a more realistic – which is to say, theoretically and empirically adequate – account of individuals as socially embedded agents, some of whom may not identify as part of the audience for comics and graphic novels. (p. 133)

A realistic portrayal of comics readers and readership is not easy to create. Small qualitative studies like the ones I have examined and my own are not conducted to be extrapolated but to provide intimate portrayals of readers. For a larger picture of this readership, researchers need to rely, for example, on sales market studies (Alverson, 2017; MacDonald, 2017) or careful extrapolations from online communities (Schenker, 2018a, 2018b). Some broad strokes emerging from these reports indicate differences in the readership depending on the sales location, the comics store or bookstore, which also correlates with gender; women tend to acquire their comics more often in bookstores (Alverson, 2017). MacDonald's analysis of the BookScan results points to an increasing diversification of the readership that both explains and supports the diversification of the comics market (2017). Analyses based on online communities should be used carefully, but they are helpful to speak about potential audiences, about readers who could be more active in digital comics consumption or who are not as visible in physical spaces. For example, the Facebook online comics community has been recently fluctuating from a majority of women to a split that is closer to even (Schenker, 2018a), therefore supporting the changes that MacDonald indicates in her BookScan analysis. These shifts make my study's composition even more relevant since more female readers participated in my interviews and self-identified as comics readers.

In conclusion, when studying readers and fans of comics, the motives and intentions of Woo (2011), Gabilliet (2010), Brown (2001), Pustz (1999), and Parsons (1991) are varied and mostly hardly comparable. But from their research one issue arises: the understudied diversity with regards to reading experiences and practices with comics and thus potential variability in the comics reading experience. Market reports are starting to indicate a demographic expansion of the readership that challenges the extended stereotype of the young male fan. The discourse about comics readership has historically been located in the analysis of these fans, their communities, and their roles and experiences. This pursuit of the fan has obscured other roles of comics as reading materials and connected reading experiences; it is time to enrich our fields of study with those experiences.

1.3 A Brief Note on Methodology

This study is guided by a hermeneutical phenomenology approach; therefore, it is qualitative in nature. As in many exploratory and inductive projects, I could not predict an end result, but I could certainly define a path to follow. This path and the relevance of this research are partly supported by a tradition of scholars who have examined the experience of pleasure reading from the reader perspective, as I have noted previously. Hermeneutic phenomenology is recommended when researchers seek to explore an experience as it is understood by those who are having it, when the topic of study is new, or it has been examined previously but a fresh perspective is needed (Cohen, Kahn, & Steeves, 2000, p. 3). The study of comics as reading material from a reader perspective is conceptualized as a new area of research, departing from the previous focus on fans as audience and comics as cultural product. As well, any research on comics readers provides a necessary new perspective lacking in library and information science (LIS), reading research, comics studies, or audience studies. The increasing visibility of comics in mainstream culture and the privileged and almost ubiquitous connection between comics reading and the fan experience makes use of this approach, and thus a fresh perspective is almost mandatory. The study also sought to privilege the readers' voices, and this approach is ideal for projects of this sort because it supports the examination of how people interpret their lives and make meaning of what they experience (Cohen et al., 2000, p. 5). Finally, it was important to approach the entire enterprise with an open mind and much curiosity; LIS scholar and supporter of the use of hermeneutic phenomenology John Budd recommends it particularly because it "opens the inquirer to possibilities instead of barricading avenues" (1995, p. 304). The themes of gender and materiality are examples of this "opening" of the inquirer. Neither of them was a part of the initial interview guide but became a part of the process after participants consistently referred to them in early stages of the interviewing process.

The approach was implemented through seventeen semi-structured interviews that sought to support the exploration of the significant and unique experiences of these readers, offering "plausible insights" (Van Manen, 1997, p. 9). Purposeful sampling supported my search for "people who offer a picture of what it is like to be themselves as they make sense of an important experience" (Cohen et al., 2000, p. 50). These interviews were the primary method of participant interaction and they made immediate the richness and multifaceted nature of the reading experience. Interviews themselves lasted between fifty minutes and two hours and were audio recorded and transcribed. The design of and approach to the interviewing process followed the guidance provided by Kvale and Brinkmann, who posit that the semi-structured lifeworld interview is based on the idea that knowledge is neither in the interviewee nor in the researcher but in the process they share where they are co-constructors of knowledge (2009, p. 109). The authors represent this idea with the concept of the "inter-view," a social and intersubjective approach to interviewing (p. 18). The process itself is close to a conversation, but because of its professional or scholarly purpose, it follows a specific pattern and technique (p. 27):

- It is semi-structured because it pursues a balance between the open everyday life conversation and the closed and fixed questionnaire.
- It uses an interview guide that provides a structure, centers the interview themes, and contains possible questions.
- Its transcription and sound recording, in combination with observations, other textual artefacts, and journal notes, constitute the materials to analyze for meaning.

In the development of the interview guide, I followed the suggestions Kvale and Brinkmann give about how to conceptualize this type of interviewing document: it includes thematic questions that help to produce knowledge and dynamic questions that help to build rapport and a relationship between interviewer and interviewee (2009, p. 131). The success of the first two questions deserves mention, especially the one about their history as comics readers, as both thematic and dynamic questions. Although I conceived of them as dynamic, they proved to be critical questions. The answers provided by the participants acted as shared knowledge, almost as building blocks, between the participants and me. We used them heavily to build rapport, and we also referred to them in comparison with answers provided to other questions. It is also important to balance abstract questions with more tangible ones, allowing the participants and me to talk about the experience of reading comics from different angles (Van Manen, 1997, pp. 66–67). The guide was modified on three occasions to add questions about reading comics in print and digital forms, a probe about gender in connection to where comics were accessed, and questions about good and bad reading experiences. I consciously considered the inclusion of these topics after the analysis of the first five interviews. These changes also correspond to the iterative design of the project.

During the interview process, my main intention was to bring a sense of acceptance, respect, and value for the experience of reading comics and what participants shared. To be able to achieve this, I also needed to be clear and transparent about my attitudes, about the way I was inquiring and seeing. Achieving clarity and transparency in my methodological work became paramount, with reflexivity as the perfect tool. Finlay points at reflexivity "as one way to begin to unravel the richness, contradictions, and complexities of intersubjective dynamics," and argues that a reflexive analysis "can only ever be a partial, tentative, provisional account" (2002, pp. 542–543). I experienced reflexivity as a process that strengthened the trustworthiness of my data and analysis as well as my contribution to other scholars who might be considering a similar methodological path. As part of this reflexive work, disclosing my own history as a comics reader was integral to revealing myself as a researcher and to building rapport with participants.

The scholarly gap I have presented, connected to my personal history as a comics reader and to the rise of comics into mainstream culture, inspired me to wonder about the status, stereotypes, and experiences related to comics reading in contemporary society and prompted the following research questions:

- What does it mean to be a comics reader in contemporary society?
- How do comics readers construct and understand their experience of comics as reading material?
- What might be learned about comics readers' identities and the social contexts of reading comics?

These questions in conjunction with a pilot study (Cedeira Serantes, 2009) guided the initial design of the recruitment tools as well as the interviewing guide. The sample included seventeen participants, from seventeen to twenty-five years of age, nine female and eight male, who also represented different reading experiences: beginning readers, occasional but committed readers, and expert readers. For the study, I attempted to recruit participants starting at fifteen years old to twenty-five years old, following the definition of youth set by the United Nations Educational, Scientific and Cultural Organization (UNESCO) (UNESCO, 2017). I recruited participants and collected data in three different sites in London (Ontario): public libraries, comics stores, and a university with a large undergraduate population. Interesting, recruiting for the younger segment was more complicated, especially in comics stores, where sometimes parents did not allow me to talk with their teens. Most participants older than eighteen were in university, with the exception of three who were part of the workforce and two who were both working and studying at the same time. Data analysis involved the following qualitative procedures: active listening, immersion in the data, data reduction and transformation, and thematic analysis (Cohen et al., 2000). The process of analysis required me to be constantly immersed in the data and to work with my own thinking process, mainly in the form of writing. I kept the connection with data through listening and transcribing. I developed both in-text and off-text notes while transcribing. Tentative themes and categories emerged from each of the interviews. I kept those themes and categories in constant dialogue with each other, allowing space for the coproduction of themes that connected aspects of their experiences as well as the development of the themes' structure. The singularity of the participants' thoughts and experiences with comics was always present and, as much as possible, highlighted in the analytical process.

Table 1 Summary of participants' background

Pseudonym	Age	Last comics read (title + main creator)	Recruitment site / Occupation	Reader status
Alison (F)	23	*Black Hole* by Charles Burns; *Scott Pilgrim* series by Bryan Lee O'Malley; and *Lucky* by Gabrielle Bell	University / Graduate student	Intermediate / Avid
Baa (M)	17	Reread *Watchmen* by Alan Moore; *Daytripper* by Fábio Moon and Gabriel Bá; and the second volume of *Phonogram* by Kieron Gillen and Jamie McKelvie	Public library / High school student	Intermediate / Avid
Daniel (M)	23	*Mome* anthology (Fantagraphics); an omnibus *Captain American* by Ed Brubaker; *Shortcomings* by Adrian Tomine; and *Torpedo* by Enrique Sánchez Abulí et al.	Comic book store / Undergraduate student, comic book store staff	Avid
Devi (F)	18	*Squee* and *I feel sick* by Jhonen Vasquez; and *Hellsing* by Kouta Hirano	University / Undergraduate student	Intermediate/ Avid
HunterS (M)	19	First three trade paperbacks in *The Sandman* series by Neil Gaiman; fifth installment of *Transmetropolitan* by Warren Ellis; and a collection of *Doctor Who* stories	University / Undergraduate student	Beginner

Jacob (M)	17	*The Wonderful Wizard of Oz* by Eric Shanower and Skottie Young; an adaptation of *Frankenstein* by Jason Cobley; and a comic in French about the history of rock and roll	Snowball sampling / High school student, library volunteer	Intermediate
Kalo (F)	24	*Filth* by Grant Morrison; *Ex-Machina* by Brian K. Vaughan; *Skim* by Mariko Tamaki and Jillian Tamaki	University / Graduate student	Avid
Lorraine (F)	19	Fifth volume of the *Wet Moon* series by Sophie Campbell; the first volume of *Akira* by Katsuhiro Otomo; and the first trade paperback of the new *Tank Girl* by Jamie Hewlett	Snowball sampling / Undergraduate student	Avid
Marian (F)	24	*Unwritten* by Mike Carey and Peter Gross and *Beast* by Marian Churchland	Public library / Intern	Avid
Oracle (F)	23	*Power Girl* with Amanda Conner as the artist; *Batgirl* by Gail Simone; and *The Muppets, the King Arthur* by Roger Langridge	University / Graduate student	Avid

Table 1 (cont.)

Pseudonym	Age	Last comics read (title + main creator)	Recruitment site / Occupation	Reader status
Preacher (M)	18	*Maus* by Art Spiegelman; *Preacher* by Garth Ennis; and *Y: The Last Man* by Brian K. Vaughan	University / Undergraduate student	Intermediate
Promethea (F)	21	Second volume of *Promethea* by Alan Moore and J. H. Williams III and *The Swamp Thing* by Alan Moore	Public market / Undergraduate student	Beginner
Selina (F)	24	*Ex-Machina* by Brian K. Vaughan; *Street Angel* by Jim Rugg and Brian Maruca; and volume one of *Strangers in Paradise* by Terry Moore	University / Graduate student, bookstore staff	Intermediate / Avid
Shade (M)	24	*The Changing Man* by Peter Milligan, but especially because of the artist, Brendon McCarthy; a single issue of *Sweet Tooth* by Jeff Lemire; and the first issue of *Flash* by Geoff Johns	Snowball sampling / IT professional	Avid
Shalmanaser (M)	20	Richard Wagner's *The Ring of the Nibelung* adapted by Roy Thomas, *Maus* by Art Spiegelman, and a collection of short stories based on H. P. Lovecraft works	Public library / IT professional	Intermediate

Templesmith (F)	20	Omnibus for *Silent Hill* by Scott Ciencin; a manga based on the television series *Battlestar Galactica*; and *Maus* by Art Spiegelman	Snowball sampling / Undergraduate student	Avid
Walker (M)	23	*V for Vendetta* by Alan Moore; the graphic novel adaptation of the animation movie *Waltz with Bashir* by Ari Folman and David Polonsky; and a Frank Miller comic he could not remember the title of	Snowball sampling / Undergraduate student	Sporadic

2 Readers and the Comics Community: What Does It Mean to Be a Comics Reader?

This section explores what defines the experience of being a reader in the midst of a culture that identifies the fan and the fan experience as the normative experience. What do I mean by *fan*? In his book *Fan Cultures*, Hills describes the fan as follows:

> It's somebody who is obsessed with a particular star, celebrity, film, TV programme, band; somebody who can produce reams of information on their object of fandom, and can quote their favoured lines or lyrics, chapter and verse. Fans are often highly articulate. Fans interpret media texts in a variety of interesting and perhaps unexpected ways. And fans participate in communal activities – they are not "socially atomised" or isolated viewers/readers. (2002, p. ix)

The participants in my study compared themselves against this experience when they attempted to define their relationship with comics and with the comics community. Especially in mainstream culture, the connection between the fan experience and comics culture has colonized the experience of reading comics, leaving almost no room for the possibility of other recognizable experiences. If you are committed to read comics, inevitably you are, will become, or are expected to become a fan. Fiske (1992) defined the boundaries of the fan experience in terms of an insider–outsider relationship. However, the diversity of experiences reflected in my participants exemplifies that these boundaries are active not just in that dichotomy but also in an in-between territory, a continuum: what is the experience of a reader who does not want to become a normative insider – a fan – but who already is more knowledgeable and involved than an outsider?

The readers in this study present different scenarios to address this question, delineating a sort of rich multilayered experience that typifies the difficulty of defining one's relationship to a certain type of media. In her remarks about research on real readers, Willis (2018) notes that real readers "are able to take up a range of different positions with respect to implied readers: subordinate, resistant, negotiated, oppositional, and so on" (p. 84). In this case, readers are not working only with or against an implied reader just in a text but also with or against an implied experience: how they read and relate to comics and the comics community. Willis's positions of subordination, resistance, negotiation, and opposition can be mapped onto my readers' descriptions. One of the best examples to initiate this discussion can be found in Alison's words regarding her own suitability to be a participant in this study:

> Actually, I wasn't sure if I should sign up for this study because I wasn't sure that I read enough ... I've read them fairly intermittently throughout my life ... there's been times when I've read a lot of them and times whe[n] I haven't ... in middle school I don't think I touched a single graphic novel ... I don't like getting anything from Heroes and I'm not familiar or super familiar with the Marvel and DC universes ... there's always people out there who read more than you.

Alison clearly expresses doubts about her adequacy to participate in the study. She hesitates because her reading and consuming practices do not fit the characteristics that define either her understanding or the pervasive understanding of what a comics reader is or does. This quote exemplifies how the experiences of fans and readers have merged in the mainstream's imagination. Even though in my recruitment tools, I neither mentioned the word *fan* nor included any superhero titles, Alison still compared her reading history and taste to those commonly expected of the comics fan. First, she questions her level of commitment because she is not a highly committed reader. Second, she neither uses the comics store nor buys comics at any other venue; her main source to access comics is the public library. Third, she says she does not know much about the two main comics publishing houses, DC and Marvel. Her last sentence, "there's always people out there who read more than you," goes full circle, returning to the idea expressed at the beginning of her statement, raising quantitative notions to challenge again her commitment to the medium but also comparing herself to an external – and always more avid – reading community. Inadvertently, Alison is responding to a very particular understanding of the comics reading experience.

Promethea has a relatively large group of friends who read comics and she clearly distinguishes two groups among them, the ones who "will read [comics] but don't expend the hours of finding the information and putting passion behind their passion" and the ones who "are those basement comic book stack collectors and [who] can tell you basically any issue from any author, from anything." Even though passionate and reflective about comics, Kalo positions herself in the middle of a continuum similar to Promethea's previous description. Kalo says, "I'm not casual, but I'm not super, super intense." Explaining his attitude toward reading, Jacob also describes a moderate approach to comics reading, showing perhaps a negative view of the fan experience through the use of the word "addicted":

> Although I've heard of people who get addicted to it and can't stop reading and stuff and [spend] a lot of time ... that's not how it is for me. I don't think that's how it would ever be just simply because that's not really what I'm looking for. I'm not

> looking to escape into the world of comic books; I just like
> comic books, like most . . . people like books.

Although Oracle defines herself as a "comic book geek" and the most avid
reader among her friends, she still compares herself to a fan community that
is very present on the Internet and that she describes as "much more
obsessive and knowledgeable." Oracle also reflected on the issue of exclu-
siveness when related to the comics community, how if too many people
like comics, they are not cool anymore, especially because "they don't like
[comics] for the right reasons." Alison, Promethea, Kalo, Jacob, and Oracle
can easily describe the two extremes of this continuum, Fiske's insider/
outsider, but they situate themselves at different points of that in-between
territory, in a position harder to describe beyond the fact that they all read
and enjoy comics.

Devi uses a different benchmark to describe herself, appealing to consumer practices: "I'm not the type that goes and buys one [single issue comics]
every week." Several readers pointed to the fact that they prefer to wait for
collected trade paperbacks rather than to buy single issues. This element of
consumer practices also emerged in relation with the use of the term *graphic
novel*, in some cases again delineating boundaries between longtime fans and
new readers. Kalo describes the tension as follows:

> I definitely feel that tension from the people who [say,] "oh, you
> just want to make it all fancy, or the fancy word for comics, why
> do you need a fancy word for comic books, why do you have to
> analyze them?" Those kinds of people who say they are just
> comic books. Because maybe those people have been reading
> them for a long time . . . of course I'm making a lot of assump-
> tions here.

Baa makes a similar observation. He believes that people use this term because they have a prejudice against comics: "you are trying to avoid something by creating this other trend, but there's nothing wrong with [comic books]." Interesting, he does not point at other readers or the comics community but to the way in which media use the term, adding one more influential layer to the process of defining oneself as part of the comics community: "when you have a story that it's not superhero related, or it's more serious, people tend to call it [a] graphic novel, for [the] BBC to quote. But to me there's no difference." Daniel recognizes a similar phenomenon. He compares it to a branding strategy where the term *graphic novel* has become representative of all comics, and therefore a term designating a format has evolved into the signifier for the entire medium. As he says, "it's this weird anomaly of branding and marketing where they've done such a good job that it becomes the thing; that is what I sort of think is happening with graphic novels." In the case of HunterS, we can see how effective this phenomenon has been. He has not been reading comics for a long time, but he defines himself more as a graphic novel reader. He defends the use of this designation because he thinks that "comic book readers are usually more . . . into the superhero stuff and usually the stuff that goes along with that, like the collectors' attitude, the memorabilia attitude." HunterS defines his comics reading in contrast to key elements of the fan experience and also closely connects the narratives published in graphic novel format to his other reading interests – science fiction with a sociopolitical angle. Basically, the term *graphic novel* has become a synonym for narratives he enjoys, as a way of filtering among the myriad materials published in comics form and perhaps distancing himself from the stereotype of the fan.

2.1 Comics Reading As Solitary and Social

Although in recent years, scholarly interest in social reading events has increased (Fuller & Rehberg Sedo, 2013; Rehberg Sedo, 2011; Long, 2003), reading has often been conceptualized and studied as a solitary activity.

The central role of fans in comics culture has always helped to conceptualize comics reading as a social activity connected to groups who create communities around physical and digital spaces such as comics stores, conventions or message boards, and publications such as fanzines or fanfiction websites. For instance, in his study of male readers of Milestone comics, Brown (2001) dedicates one chapter to focus on eight individual readers between nine and seventeen years old. Brown's analysis focuses on masculinity and identity and through that process, we also get to see other elements that are part of the reading lives or media landscape of these readers, for example, how comics stores and conventions are important spaces in relation to comics reading (pp. 103–128). Looking back to past comics readers practices, Tilley (2014) advises present librarians about the potential that the participatory culture that emerges around comics reading has to support creativity and civic engagement.

The participants in my study offer a wide array of scenarios and experiences that strongly expand the conceptualization of comics reading as both individual and communal. Lorraine sees fan-based engagement as subject to the influence of the larger community and, in her particular case, as a sort of "companionship." Conversely, reading itself is defined as private and individual:

> [About readers: Reading is] something even more of an indivi-dualistic experience. A reader is going to keep reading; it doesn't matter if it's uncool or a lot of people aren't doing it. That's their interest and they're confident in that way. A fan is someone sort of like me, [who] like[s] that companionship, that sense of community.

Selina delves into the idea of reading as something solitary. Reading creates moments for her "to just be invested in my own thing." She is not surrounded by comics readers either, with the exception of her sister, so sharing is not a primary activity connected to reading. A different view is held by Preacher, who recognized a priceless duality. In alignment with Selina, he describes reading comics as something "sort of therapeutic" and he looks for privacy and quietness to read because "you want just to immerse yourself." He complemented this classic depiction of solitary reading by praising the possibility of conversing about comics because "[it] can help you to find better comics, can make you think about things you didn't know you read, the significance, the underline, the subtext of a story that you didn't even pick up on; someone can tell you that." He concluded this reflection with the thought that "the social aspect is a great part of it but not necessary." The idea of social reading as something optional can be one factor that helps to explain the different stages that a reader can undergo in her reader history, as we see in the case studies I present next about two comics readers, Marian and Daniel.

Marian recalled this social aspect of reading as part of her adolescent experience. She developed an informal reading club for manga with two friends, where each of them was in charge of a different manga genre. As she explains it:

> I was the boy's love "specialist" and then this other girl had
> mainly really classic ones and then this other girl had romantic
> ones 'specially and another one had more edgy or darker
> vampire type of things.

Although currently she described herself more as a solitary reader, this activity was primary in her social life during high school. Membership in a group like this, as with any book club, can potentially affect the way one reads a comic since reading is done both for oneself and for sharing with the other group members. Although I share Daniel's experiences at length later, his thoughts about social reading are relevant to highlight here. Daniel described reading as primarily social during his childhood and early adolescence; his reading became more private as he grew older, but he does still feel part of something larger, a "subculture," defined by comics reading. As he explains it, "100 percent of the population watches movies, 80–90 percent of the population listens to music . . . what percent of the population reads comics?" Thus comics reading becomes a distinctive practice, one that creates difference for Daniel because he sees it as not yet completely embraced by mainstream society. This conceptualization that Daniel describes is similar to Preacher's experience where comics reading can be both solitary and social.

These perspectives complicate the comics reading experience since it is described as not just a social event that allows the individual to be part of a fan community, but also as a private activity that then becomes social for diverse reasons, including the need for sharing, for discussion to understand, or for companionship.

2.2 Female Readers and Comics: Selina and Promethea

Comics have not always been dominated by a male audience. At the height of their popularity during the 1940s, funny animals, teen humor, and romance comics made this medium popular with both adolescent and preadolescent boys *and* girls (Gabilliet, 2010, pp. 31–32; Wright, 2003, pp. 127–128). The research work of cartoonist Trina Robbins is invaluable to study and understand the topics of girls' comics and female creators, both in the mainstream and in underground comics (2013, 1999), but perhaps her focus on creators and texts leaves the examination of audiences and readers secondary. The scholarly landscape in the United Kingdom with regards to girls' comics and girl readers is rather different, as the work of Mel Gibson shows (2015, 2008). Gibson connects her scholarly project to a lineage of British scholars who looked at popular culture and female consumers, such as the influential work of Angela

McRobbie (1991). From Gibson's productive scholarship, the two works I highlight concentrate on UK postwar comics, especially girls' comics, up until the 1980s and the memories of adult readers regarding their childhood cultural practices around them. For comics to be acceptable and purchased, especially by gatekeepers, they had to be gender appropriate, making the activity of swapping essential for girls to get exposed to other types of comics and, in some cases, come to reject the genre of girls' comics (2008, pp. 158–161). Being a female reader of comics was a contested identity, since it could be "liberating" but also "problematic in terms of gender" (p. 166) and, in the case of female readers who read across gender lines, even "transgressive" (2015, p. 185).

In comparison with the UK market, where girls' comics disappeared from the cultural landscape relatively late in the 1990s, in the American market, teen humor comics (with the exception of Archie) and romance comics vanished from the market in the 1970s. Since then, North American comics culture has become predominantly male territory and female readers and fans are, more often than not, outsiders to this readership and this community. The situation is definitely changing, as some scholars have noted in their research about female fans or *fangirls* (e.g., Orme, 2016; Busse, 2013; Scott, 2013). Interesting, these scholarly projects focus more on the fan experience, leaving Nyberg's (1995) book chapter "Comic books and women readers: Trespassers in masculine territory?" as one of the only recognizable works in the North American context that looks at women readers who "find pleasure in comics books, a form of popular culture that seems to appeal almost exclusively to a masculine audience" (p. 213).

Describing the experience of female readers still simply as outsiders in comics culture would be simplifying a rather complicated experience. Nyberg refers to her discussants as "trespassers" because that term points to the way in which "they treat the constructed gender boundaries as 'fluid' and trespass both in the text and in a more physical sense by their participation in the process of purchasing and reading comics" (1995, p. 213). I see mine as *squatters*: most of them have been part of comics culture for some time, but generally they are not seen as legitimate members yet. They are searching for a balance where they become part of comics culture, but in that process, they also actively want to change it and carve out their own space. This change can be in contrast with Nyberg's work (1995) where she actively looked for women readers, while female participants responded to this study as readers of comics, not as women readers or fangirls. In this section, Promethea and Selina offer some contrasting positions in their relationship with comics reading and culture, but the voices of other readers are also heard about topics such as the role of knowledge in the process of becoming/being recognized comics readers; their awareness of and difficulty in finding satisfactory female characters and creators; the negotiation of male-dominated readerly spaces; and the role of other female readers in the introduction to the format.

One of the most rewarding aspects of the interviewing process with Selina was witnessing her journey of self-discovery dealing with being a female comics reader and her relationship with comics culture. For example, she soon realizes some of the conflicting positions she holds: she thinks that the comics community – especially the superheroes community – is rather inaccessible for beginners, but at the same time, she wishes to be part of it:

> I'm sitting here criticizing what I think is maybe the access point to a medium as being extraordinary inaccessible. So here I am criticizing this, but then I'm going on about how I really have to be precise about this and the other thing, which is all, I think, evidence of the fact I have this unbelievable impulse to fit into that thing.

To be able to fit in and participate in this community, knowing is strongly connected to community construction and identification. Selina compares it to what happens in other fan communities: "with Trekkies or with graphic novels or with whatever, everybody . . . had to sort of defend their interest." Hence for her the need to know about her object of interest goes beyond mere personal interest and it becomes an issue of community construction and boundaries. Knowledge acquisition becomes an external imposition, and she feels like "I need to know everything"; not knowing makes her feel like an outsider.

I have situated the analysis of the interaction between knowing and becoming/being a reader as part of the gender analysis because it emerged primarily among female participants. Male participants, like Preacher or Baa, also raise knowledge as relevant but less important. Baa defines himself as "an avid comic book reader" at the same time that he recognizes a gap in his knowledge, especially about the superhero industry before he started reading comics. For Preacher, being a fan and knowing about comics go hand in hand: "If I want to say I'm a comic book fan I should know sort of the origins and the style of the most influential authors." Female participants showed a heightened sensitivity to the value of knowledge as a signifier of status in their constant struggle to be admitted as part of the community. Similarly to Baa, Kalo also mentions this idea of constantly catching up, but her case needs a larger contextualization. She started to read comics in her adolescence. Her access to popular culture in general, and to comics and young adult literature in particular, was restricted by her parents' hegemonic understanding of reading: school related, productive, and done with something that looked like "real novels." At sixteen/seventeen she connected with a group of friends whom she describes as "nerdy." Although she was mainly a solitary reader, for Kalo, the process of discovering comics was part of a larger process of introduction to new media, a new student community, and the exploration of the nerd/geek identity:

> But for me, I was kind of like having a cultural awakening
> at [that] time of my life and I was trying to take in as much
> culture as I can. I don't know if it was conscious or not, but
> that was definitely what I was doing. I was listening to
> music I have never heard before, watching movies that
> I've never watched, and … my friends were like "you got
> to read these comics."

Although adolescence might seem a young age to begin reading comics, Kalo thought that it was already too late and she felt like she had to catch up, realizing immediately that "that wasn't going to happen, I would need at least three lifetimes to try to catch up with some of these stories that have been going on … they are like soap operas!" She is also one of the participants who better explains the usefulness, almost necessity, of studying comics, since she took a university course about comics and graphic novels at the University of Toronto. This helped her to define and expand her taste and equipped her with a rigorous approach to reading comics.

In the case of Devi and Promethea, the function that comics knowledge played in the construction of their identities as readers and their sense of belonging to the community is notable and rather complex. Again, a conflict emerges from the dissonance between how participants perceive themselves as readers and who they think they need to be in order to be perceived as such by the community and to be part of it. Although they are committed to the medium, they do not know enough to consider themselves part of this imagined reading community. On one hand, Devi believes that one should know about creators because they deserve acknowledgment/recognition and she regrets not being more knowledgeable about publishers. On the other hand, she talks about the "comic book snobs," groups of readers who are easily recognizable at conventions because of their judgmental attitudes. She would also like to participate in in-depth conversations about comics and feels knowledge is clearly needed to have an informed discussion. She reflects about how she sees her future role in this community: "I possibly, I wouldn't shut anyone down like I see those people are doing, but . . . I think once I get more into the culture I'll have an opinion and I want to voice [it]. I like debating. And if someone reads the same things, going back and forward, it would be interesting." Even though she can be considered a rather knowledgeable reader, Devi still perceives her place as that of an outsider because she does not fit the expectations to be able to be an insider and active participant. She sees her future participation in these conversations as a tool to bring change and openness to the community. Finally, for Promethea, the need to know does not make her feel like an outsider. Even though she recognizes she does not have a lot of knowledge about comics, especially in comparison to some of her friends, as I explain in the following, her comfort visiting and being at the comics store makes her already feel part of the community. However, she still expresses a strong feeling about her lack of knowledge: "I'm really bad with names and titles. I hate it; it makes me feel so useless." Her sense of self-worth seems to be partially linked to knowledge. Her passion for the medium, her admiration for members who possess vast knowledge, and her declared eagerness to learn are not enough to avoid the feeling of being "useless."

As I have introduced, knowledge is a powerful element to influence the sense of belonging to the comics community. Perhaps a more tangible element is the physical space of the comics store. Going back to Woo's research, he describes comics stores as institutions that sustain comic book culture and that are "integral" to its reproduction in North America (Woo, 2011, pp. 133–134). If we consider comics stores from that perspective, they become settings where different practices are perpetuated or challenged, not just simply places to access comics. Based on Goffman, Woo explains how visitors can see the store as a "sanctuary" or see themselves as part of a "team"; however, the insertion of gender can challenge Woo's theorizing. Kalo describes how female readers are constantly reminded of their differences:

> You'd walk into a comic book store, everyone working there is male, and you walk in with a group of males and maybe some- one will [say], "uh, you're the only girl in this store," one of those things ... it was never an issue. I don't take them seriously.

Consequently, for women readers, the idea of the store as a "sanctuary" disappears, almost becoming a fighting ring, a place of struggle and affirmation. Two initiatives indicate a tendency for this status to change and make comics stores spaces that are welcoming for women and any marginalized community. For example, the Geek Initiative, an online community focused on supporting equality in geek communities, maintains a webpage that lists comics stores that are described as inclusive by their readers (Geek Initiative, 2018). In 2015, Panels, the comics-focused section of Book Riot, dedicated a post to highlight female-owned comics stores in the United States (Schenkel, 2015) and in the same year, Ariell Johnson created Amalgam Comics & Coffeehouse, "the only black-woman owned shop of its kind, and the first black-woman owned comic book store on the East Coast" (Amalgam, 2018). These developments are encouraging, but there is still much to change.

Templesmith is a frequent visitor to one of the comics stores in the city. She compliments the store and the staff and has a comprehensive knowledge of the store's stock. However, she also recognizes that she has been at the receiving end of comments that, for example, stereotype her comics taste as a female reader with phrases such as "the *Astro Boy* section is in the back" in reference to the preference of female readers for manga titles. Even though she has considerable knowledge about comics titles and creators, Oracle also felt rather self-conscious asking for help because she thought her taste was constantly being scrutinized. From this insecurity emerges an overall issue where the store is perceived as a place where the fan – with an expected gender and level of knowledge – seems to be the only customer welcomed. In spite of the aforementioned initiates, the acceptance is not yet unconditional. In 2017, during NY Comic Con, one of the most talked about stories was a heated discussion that emerged in the panel that Marvel editors led for an audience of comic book retailers (Marston, 2017). The cause of the discussion was a complaint from one retailer about the ethnic, gender, and sexual orientation changes in recognized characters such as Thor (becoming a woman) or Iron Man (being black). Although the discussion was initiated by one retailer, reporting indicates that the issue provoked both positive and negative reactions, which just might be one indicator of the in-flux state of comics culture.

Selina unequivocally states that "as a female I feel particularly uncomfortable in comics stores," but quickly starts unfolding this statement especially in connection to the old site for The Beguiling, a store in Toronto. This comics store had two floors, the first floor where customers could find alternative/independent comics, fanzines, art books, and children's comics, and the second one where one could find more single issues from the big publishers like DC, Marvel, and Image, as well as mainstream manga. While she is explaining these spaces, Selina expresses an interest in working at a comics store, and, although as a customer she feels more comfortable in spaces like the first floor, she would prefer to work on the second floor to make it "more accessible for people." On each of the floors, Selina sees represented a different cluster of comics culture, the second floor encapsulating the traditional comics culture, with superhero characters, convoluted storylines, and male fans and staff:

> I don't know the name of every title, I don't know the name of every single issue, I don't know the entire story arc of Batman per specific author, I don't know all of these things; it doesn't mean that I don't want to know, but I feel because I don't know that stuff that particularly male employees look down on me that way.

In contrast with all these issues, she comments on the possibility of opening a store in Toronto run just by women where customers could comfortably show their inexperience or ignorance about these superhero narratives. For example, she explains that a customer could come to the store and say: "I'm totally interested in reading about Batman. I don't know where to start, and I don't know all the story arcs, but I want to start somewhere and then move forward." But the presence of female employees would not be the final solution to her discomfort at the comics store since she also says that "I would never go to The Beguiling and ask that, ever! Even if there was a female working there, never!" She did recall a satisfactory experience with a female staff member at The Beguiling, and during that recollection, she connected her discomfort with male employees to her own self-perception as a beginner reader, connecting the conversation of gender to a problem of perceptions and expectations imposed explicitly through the comic book culture and especially at the comics store:

> For me, I would say more than anything … it would be my own lack of confidence on my knowledge and so I can say that I will feel … my experience has led me to feel particularly uncomfortable asking a male comic book or graphic novels, no, only comic books, a comic book employee a question generally.

In contrast with the complicated layer of self-understanding in Selina's case, Promethea's is especially interesting because of its singularity. She tries to visit the store as often as her busy schedule allows, sometimes to purchase comics and at other times simply to sit on the floor and read. When I asked her about her level of comfort visiting the store, she first expressed surprise about the inquiry itself, saying that "I can't believe that that's even a problem for you to be asking me a question." She immediately praised the staff and highlighted her relationship with one particular employee, whom she described as "an amazing person" and "the bomb." When I mentioned to her that other female participants expressed certain uneasiness with the predominantly male presence in comics stores and shared the fear of being judged or singled out, she recalled a conversation with a female friend whose experience was not as pleasant as hers. Interesting, Promethea first indicates that behavior like that can be experienced anywhere. "That's an everyday thing, not even within comic book stuff; you find that everywhere." She is not oblivious to the possibility of sexism, but she still cannot believe something like this happened at the store she often visits. Staff often develop these personal relationships with frequent customers who have pull lists and visit the store weekly and with whom they have conversations about plots, characters, or particular titles. During my time visiting and recruiting at different stores, I witnessed some of these interactions. However, Promethea does not fit this profile either. She does not mention comics as the catalyst for the development of this personal connection with staff, nor does she describe the store as a preferred place to socialize or talk about comics. It seems that the comfort she experiences comes from treating the store as any other space. She is not actively trying to fit into comics culture. She is definitely not uncomfortable with her position as a beginner reader and does not show any concern about asking questions or having to demonstrate any knowledge about comics. Perhaps the case of Promethea serves as a positive exception that might help researchers to further examine the metamorphosis of the comics store. The role of this place can potentially become less defined because of the diversification process in its clientele as well as the content and publishing formats of comics. The store is still mainly perceived and perpetuated as the place for the committed male fan, but beginner readers and female readers are visiting comics stores with different expectations. Thus previous dynamics might be, at least, questioned.

The gendering of the comics stores is also noticeable when the participants talk about reading mentors and their first memories about comics. Daniel recalled how his father would be the one taking him to the comics store. Conversely, the context of his first time reading comics involved his mother buying him comics at a convenience store:

> It would happen in the summer when my family would go up to
> my mother's cottage. There was a general store there, and they
> have one of those spinner racks, and if I could read the comic to
> my mother, she would give me money to go and buy another.

Often the memories that involved mothers or sisters tended to be connected to everyday activities like grocery shopping and mostly away from the space of the comics store. Unquestionably, society understands reading as a predominately female activity. Among other factors, this feminization of reading is often raised to justify the lack of interest that boys have in reading. In contrast, comics reading is predominantly described and understood as a male activity. In my project, fathers, brothers, and male friends are often mentioned as the ones introducing my participants to comics reading. But the increasing importance of mothers, sisters, and female friends should not be ignored. In her dissertation, Snowball (2011) highlights family as the main source for reading materials: teens found books to read among their home collections (p. 196) or books were being passed around among siblings (p. 67). Note that one of

Snowball's participants, Sandra, mentioned that her interest for graphic novels grew from her mother's love for the medium. In the case of my study, female readers clearly became advocates for reading in general and comics reading in particular. Interestingly, Gibson (2008) also reports on one of her interviewees, Judy, who as an adult continued to acquire and share comics with her children (p. 154). Daniel, Selina, Devi, and Promethea described similar scenes when I asked them about their first memories about comics reading: they recounted moments when their mothers bought them comics to encourage their reading.

Selina also mentioned buying comics with her mother and her sister at the grocery store and compares her taste with her sister's, who "[is] obsessed and she knows all the story arcs that [the character] Wonder Woman ever had," and who buys single issues of television adaptations like *Buffy* (1999–) and *Angel* (2000–2002). But as we saw with Daniel, this influence is not exclusive with female readers. In the case of HunterS, his comics reading has been impacted by female readers. His mother and sister's interest in comics was developed later in life, but it has been crucial to change HunterS's perspective on comics and to support his reading interest. They encouraged HunterS to explore titles such as *The Sandman* (1991–1997) or *V for Vendetta* (1989). His girlfriend is also a comics reader, and she often recommends titles to him. Although Jacob inherited Spiderman comics from his dad, he also highlighted his mother's role in supporting any kind of reading and especially at not judging his interest in comics. Also, a female friend of his sister is the person with whom he shares his interest for comics the most. In Jacob's case, it is important to mention that his mother is a librarian and similarly to Walker, her role in encouraging reading in general is especially significant. Although some of these scenarios might reinforce a general role of women as supporters of reading, one should not deny the potential influence that women recommending comics can have in blurring the boundaries around the activity of reading in general and the exclusivity of comics reading as a male activity in particular.

2.3 *The Metamorphosis of a Comics Reader: Alison and Daniel*

As mentioned in the introductory section, comics reading was historically described as something that readers eventually "grow out of," thus constructing this kind of reading experience as transient, trivial, visible only in passing, and often defined by lower levels of investment or engagement. Readers are often included in the group of fans for whom experiencing media texts is something "among many of their hobbies that do not shape their identity and that may be temporarily limited" (Busse & Gray, 2011, p. 431). In contrast with these perspectives, my participants' reflections open a door for a more complex and richer conceptualization, that their reading engagement with comics can be broadened, cultivated, diverse, and cumulative. For this, I focus on two readers, Daniel and Alison, both with different personal stories and past and present engagement with comics.

Above all, Alison is a reader. Comics are neither her main nor her unique source for reading experiences. Her attraction for poetry and her permanent questioning about her status as a comics reader are distinctive characteristics of her participation. She identifies Drawn & Quarterly and Fantagraphics as her favorite publishers. As favorite authors, she talks about Chris Ware, Daniel Clowes, Neil Gaiman, Alison Bechdel, Ariel Schrag, and Craig Thompson. She also reads webcomics such as *xkcd*, *Achewood*, and *Girls with Slingshots*, but she tends not to follow them regularly. She points to an illustrated Bible as her first memory of reading anything that was illustration heavy. As a child, she used to spend summers in Germany and recalls reading *Donald Duck* and *Alf* in German because her language skills were not very strong. Alison "thought they were lesser than the classic fiction," but her exposure to other titles later on provoked the overcoming of this stereotypical understanding. In tenth grade, she encountered *Maus* by Art Spiegelman, which became a signpost in her reading history. After that, she says, she did not stop reading comics. Another memorable moment was reading *Persepolis* by Marjene Satrapi as part of a common reading program for incoming university students. It is relevant to discuss two issues in regards to the selection of a graphic novel for these reading programs. First, these programs have become relatively common on North American campuses (and on some UK campuses) to help freshmen transition into college life and especially to help foster a sense of community (Ferguson, Brown, & Piper, 2014), thus recognizing and attempting to utilize social reading among young people. Second, choosing graphic novels in an educational environment is not without controversy. In 2013, *Persepolis* itself was pulled from some Chicago schools (Comic Book League Defense Fund, 2018a) and in 2014, *Fun Home* was core to a case where its inclusion in a voluntary summer reading program for incoming freshmen at the College of Charleston provoked the South Carolina General Assembly to consider budget cuts against that college (Comic Book League Defense Fund, 2018b). At the same time that these titles are attacked in secondary and postsecondary institutions, other scholars are pointing at the power of graphic novels as the new Bildungsroman (Schwarz & Crenshaw, 2011) or are using them in the classroom as successful coming-of-age stories that inspire students to create their own (Hughes, King, Perkins, & Fuke, 2011).

Alison's work at a bookstore supported her comics reading habits and exposure to new titles, but currently the library is her primary source for comics. For most of her life, Alison was a solitary reader. Despite developing a taste for comics in university, she never had a group of people around her with whom to share her comics reading. At the time of the interview, she had recently connected to a group of comics readers and she was enjoying the recommendations and discussions they had. This is an informal group that she described as diverse and without hierarchies. She also accentuated the fact that there are other female members. She even connected her recent increase in comics reading to the influence of this group. In regards to comics stores, she said that they "feel like there's a lot of men in them but it's not ... I've never felt uncomfortable in them." When I asked her to expand on that thought, she connected this neutral experience to her minimal interaction with staff. She uses the space as a place to browse, to discover new titles that she then will look for at the library. For Alison, knowledge is something connected to any reading experience; she sees herself as an informed reader and wants to be able to be one with respect to her comics reading. For this she consults different sources for information about authors before and after reading their work. Looking closer at plotlines and genres, Alison expressed an interest in how manga generally allows certain gender fluidity in its stories and characters. She talked about the manga genre Yaoi/Boy's love with curiosity because most creators and readers are women. She commented more specifically on the fact that women enjoy reading this genre even though the main two protagonists are male, but recognizes that this peculiarity might allow women to explore either role in the romantic relationship, thus expanding and experimenting with gender, sexuality, and sex roles. In contrast with her prose reading, she identified the slice-of-life as a genre that explores more in comics:

> There're some things, certain genres in graphic novels that I don't feel like I really see or even enjoy in prose ... I really liked *Lucky* and I really liked Ariel Schrag stuff, which it probably comes off as really annoying and whiny in prose.

Finally, when talking about comics as a narrative medium, she highlighted a difference in her relationship with the text, especially in contrast with reading prose. Alison defines herself as a conscientious reader, and the lessening or lack of text in comics opens new possibilities in her reading experience. She says that the lack of text makes her "stop and notice the art a little bit more and it also makes me try to get inside the characters' heads a little bit more because they're not telling me what they're thinking." In contrast, when reading prose, "I have trouble stopping myself. . . and thinking about what I'm reading or thinking about what the characters are thinking that the author is not telling us because they'll describe [their] movements . . . or gestures; it's harder."

Daniel was one of the most experienced readers and at the time of the interview also worked part time at a comics store. Daniel's comics reading experience started as a leisure activity, as I previously mentioned, supported by his mother, who bought him comics to encourage his reading habit. As he grew up, Daniel kept reading comics and started to focus primarily on superhero titles. Buying and reading comics also shifted into a social activity that he shared with friends. However, his relationship with comics changed during adolescence. Reading comics had to compete for time and attention with other new interests like skateboarding. Reading comics lost its social and public status and became an individual and private activity. During those years, he became an avid reader and his interest for collecting comics became even more intense. This intensity also created a problem. The financial commitment of buying comics and his loss of interest for superhero comics almost made him abandon the medium. He carefully explains it:

> When I was in high school, it was just a lot. It was a financial
> issue; it was a lot of money to be spending on the same thing.
> I was very close minded to the medium; I was just reading the
> superhero stories, and after a while you start to think . . . super-
> hero stories are great, but when that's all you read, it can take its
> toll – the same sort of story, plot, there's a villain, there's a hero,

there's something in between. There [just] wasn't enough
variety in what I was reading, and that's one of the reasons,
other than financial, that I was sort of . . . that I drifted away
a little bit. But once you get really engulfed by the medium,
[and] you see the vastly different things that people are doing
with it, then there's no going back.

Daniel clearly remembers that he was not exposed to "the vastly different
things that people are doing with [comics]" until he started to work at the
comics store. The owner introduced him to alternative titles like Chester
Brown's *I Never Liked You*. Daniel recognized that his understanding and
knowledge about comics was very narrow. At the same time, he was not sure
if his teen self would have enjoyed these alternative comics "because of the type
of person I was and my mind-set at the time." These words explain very simply
the idea that sometimes there is a time for certain reading materials. Daniel now
considers comics an important part of his life and defines his relationship with
them as "more than just leisure and entertainment," at the same time expressing
that he "wouldn't say that I'm a slave to them." Although his work at the
comics store and his diverse and considerable knowledge would situate
Daniel's identity closer to that of the fan, he still wants to distinguish his
relationship with comics by noting that it is one among others.

   In the end, what we see in these readers' stories is that their development
as readers and their relationship with comics reading is multifaceted since taste,
engagement, and commitment can change under many different circumstances.
A reading history with comics can start with Archie comics or with superhero
stories. It might start either as a social or a solitary activity to shift later on to the
opposite. In most cases, readers enjoy and question the medium and appreciate
and want the diversity that it can offer. Basically, these experiences also support
the idea that readers do not need to "grow out of" but "grow with" comics.

3 The Reading Experience: Encountering Comics As Reading Material

In an interview with *Comics Journal*, science fiction writer Samuel R. Delany defined the reader of comics as a "co-producer of the comics text at a level of involvement and intensity just through the nature of the medium itself" (Delany & Groth, 1979, p. 40). Delany is strongly defending an active role for the reader in the process of reading, locating also the nature of this active association in the comics language. In the process of explaining his approach to the medium of comics as the "art of tensions," comics scholar Charles Hatfield (2009, 2005) also critically reflects about the relationship between text and reader. Because of the different tensions intrinsic to the comics language, from the reader's perspective, "comics would seem radically fragmented and unstable. Therefore comics readers must call upon different reading strategies, or interpretative schema, than for the reading of conventional written text" (Hatfield, 2009, p. 132). Speaking of these strategies, Daniel explains them in terms of a synergy, of realizing and enjoying the complementary relationship between text and art:

> You can read a comic quickly, but you're not necessarily reading it at all. With comics I try not to go too quickly because you're not taking everything in; there's a lot of visual information there, [and] it's almost like reading between the lines of a novel. No, I wouldn't say text or images are more important than the other. I think there's a synergy between the two of them and when reading comics, sequential fiction, or nonfiction, you have to be conscious of that and you have to realize that they're complementary, not contradictive, if that makes sense.

Readers' agency and medium complexity work together to make readers feel like they are both being challenged but still have control over the experience. In contrast with the discourses of comics as light or easy reading, Scott McCloud highlights readers' agency when he theorizes the importance of the gutter in the reading experience, calling "the reader an equal partner in crime" (1994, p. 68). Likewise for Templesmith, the crucial role of "the space between the panels" – the gutter – cannot be denied, "and it's weird with comic books because it's not the same with regular books; when you pause between frames and you think about the scene and how it plays out, that I love." For her, the gutter is the place where thinking happens and allows her even more enjoyment.

But not all the decisions are based on medium affinity. Along with agency and complexity, something as common as genre preference also influences comics reading. When we discussed the developments in Alison's reader history, she mentioned her affinity for reading slice-of-life stories written in comics. Marian and Baa agreed with this view that certain stories or genres work better for them as comics. Both readers talked about the same title, *Scott Pilgrim* (2004–2010), but they chose it for different reasons. Marian said about it that "it really works" and that it is "just fun." It is a type of narrative that she often reads in comics form, but she is not equally inclined to read it as a novel. In contrast, Baa praises the "humor" and the combination of "simplicity" and "the profound story" conveyed in *Scott Pilgrim*. As he says: "I think it's so deep, so beautiful, and a lot of people think that it's simple, just a story, but you can take so much from it." These initial discussions start to define a web of elements that makes comics attractive to these readers, hinting already at a complex reading experience. The mix of text and image and what it provokes is already one of the most salient characteristics and, as Preacher says, is what makes difficult stories "more accessible," "enjoyable," and "appealing." This duality of quick and intense engagement without losing storyline complexity is highlighted by different readers.

As part of the interview, I asked my participants to tell me about a reading that they enjoyed and one they did not. This question was intended to create a space where my participants could talk about the moment when they are reading and what makes some reading events satisfying and others not so much. What I understand as the reading event refers to the instance when text and reader encounter each other. I first trace the reasoning behind the intent of focusing on this particular back to de Certeau (1984). Since Jenkins's work (1992) about fans as "poachers," de Certeau is often called to explain the productive reading of fans, but his work more generally helped to see readers as active contributors in reading, not mere receptors of the text. In the process of exploring how readers become producers and reading an active practice, de Certeau explains how text and reader relate in "an interplay of implications and ruses between two sorts of 'expectation' in combination" (p. 170); those expectations are the ones of the readable space – the text – and the actual reading of the text – the practices and concrete interpretations by a reader (p. 171). Comics as texts arrive in the hands of readers bearing certain characteristics beyond the narrative they contain, such as production or cultural value. The reader also comes with a history, assumptions, desires, and expectations. I attempt to keep my focus on the interplay between the text and the reader, looking to explore salient characteristics or elements that positively or negatively define this interplay in the context of comics reading.

One of the first difficulties my participants and I encountered was that it was not easy to speak about this interplay, about this aspect of the reading experience. As Balling (2016) explains in her chapter theorizing the reading experience, the difficulty of verbalizing this experience emerges from the fact that it "is not only a linguistic phenomenon but also a phenomenological and psychological phenomenon that besides cognitive, rational, conceived experiences includes sensuous and unconscious layers of meaning" (p. 50). Baa offered us an example of this difficulty. As part of a longer reflection exploring why reading comics is different from consuming other media, he said that "it's a feeling, literally, that you get from reading [comics]. And the more I get this feeling when I'm reading them, the more I like the comics." He could not elaborate on this feeling much further, but this idea of comics inspiring a certain state, a certain sensation, is the most satisfactory way of describing it for him. And he is not alone in using these terms. Kalo expressed the same difficulty in characterizing this feeling and added to her explanation a particular mood she tends to be in when she chooses comics. Interesting, this issue of the different feeling kept coming back throughout the interview, even staying with her later as she reached out after the interview to elaborate on it:

> Although this seems like a simplistic way of looking at this, I thought about it for a while, and this is the best I can come up with. It's just a "feeling," so it's very hard to explain why I sometimes read comic books and other times novels. It has nothing to do with a specific emotion (e.g., I don't read comic books only when I'm happy), but sometimes, it seems to have to do with how much time I have. I'm a very slow reader, no matter what I'm reading, but comic books are slightly quicker than novels for me. So sometimes my choice of a comic book over a novel is based on convenience (e.g., how much time I have on hand), and at other times, I make a decision based on a "feeling" that I can't really explain other than the desire to be stimulated visually.

Kalo suggested two intertwined reasons to read comics, both connected with her own characteristics as a reader. The experience of time, personal and social, emerged repeatedly when talking about comics reading. Participants mentioned having time to read and the different rhythms that comics reading permits as primary issues in relation to choosing comics as reading material.[3] In research about reading habits and youth, the study of time management and distribution is not uncommon, especially since the eruption of new technologies in the media landscape. Time is at a premium, and the societal fear is that youth is abandoning leisure reading and embracing a combination of video-game playing, video watching, and smartphone socializing. Especially among college students, studies address such topics as the influence of reading time on academic achievements, on the improvement of literacy skills, and on the distribution of time among competing media practices (Mokhtari, Reichard, & Gardner, 2009; Hughes-Hassell & Rodge, 2007; Johnsson-Smaragdi & Jönsson, 2006; Gallik, 1999).

The second reason to choose comics for Kalo is based on her affinity for the visual component of comics. Note that for a long time, this visual element has often been used to qualify comics as not *true* reading, something that has slowly changed in the past ten years as comics have been strongly connected to the development of visual and multimodal literacies (Botzakis, Savitz, & Low, 2017). Before we move to the sections examining successful and challenging reading experiences, Selina offers the following thought that accurately summarizes this initial discussion:

> I think graphic novels for me sort of combine the intellectual necessary participation with the "I don't have to think as much," but then, my second impulse is to say that's rudimentary and that's not actually how I feel because I feel that there's a lot

---

[3] For a closer examination of the topic of time and comics reading, please see Cedeira Serantes (2016) and Sabeti (2012b).

of graphic novels that are actually really challenging to engage with . . . I'm trying to think of something . . . but anyway, there are some that are like, I would never say that, it's incredibly challenging to participate in the structure or the format or the art, or something like that, so I'm not really sure what I'm saying now . . . I'm having so many epiphanies.

Selina was not afraid of sharing her struggle at defining what makes comics reading different. In her effort to unpack her passion for comics, Selina came to terms with the fact that, at the same time, comics can seem easy to read but also be challenging. This duality could be connected to the medium merge of text and visual elements that overall seems to support a very particular, unique, and often preferable reading experience.

3.1 Rereading, Satisfaction, and Boredom in the Comics Reading Experience

As Mackey's continuous exploration of media, reading, and youth (2011, 2007a) shows, there is still room for development and analysis. Baa emphasized his need and interest for the comics reading experience when, after he described the medium as "magical" and shared the "overwhelming power" that comics have with him, he concluded: "I don't know if you can put it in words." However, two concepts, rereading and satisfaction, help to define a successful reading experience. Participants have used these two elements in combination: satisfaction tends to be a reason to reread a comic and the impulse to reread a particular work becomes an indication that it provides a satisfactory experience.

As we have seen, comics are reading materials that participants strongly relate to reading for pleasure. Devi used them as a break from all the reading she does in her English degree. Preacher said that reading comics "it's just interesting; I can enjoy it, I get surprised, I'll laugh, I'll cry, you know. I think it's much more fun to read a comic." He found comics "sort of therapeutic" when he is worried or stressed. However, again reading for pleasure does not mean easy or simplistic reading:

> With the comic you are really working to understand it. You have to read every word and interpret it and make connections, oh this character was here, oh this guy needs this. With a movie you can just sort of tune out and let it play.

So, how then do these participants decide if they are actually enjoying their reading experience? In her study of reading/playing in different formats, Mackey (2007a) shares the concepts of salience and fluency as crucial in the process that her participants follow to select among different texts (pp. 88–92). Participants in her study judged each text according to its own characteristics and the merits of the format, and they decided which materials to read based on interest (salience) or familiarity with the medium (fluency). In the case of my participants, these two elements are already implicit in their reflections. They often highlight the unique narratives and storytelling that they find in comics in comparison with other media, and their self-selection as comics readers indicates that the medium itself is salient. Also, even though the study mixes beginner, intermediate, and avid readers, all of them share a level of familiarity and ease with the medium. Therefore a question emerges: if saliency and fluency are factors already present among participants, what other factors or elements do they use to define their reading experiences with comics? The concept of satisfaction and the action of rereading help to explore this question and are especially helpful to see how readers decide that a certain comic or a certain reading experience is truly pleasurable.

In relation to rereading, first I would like to address the participants who shared that they did not reread. Their hesitation was not based on a different understanding of the medium or the reading process but on an external factor, lack of time. Again, time availability becomes an important factor. Both Alison and Daniel declared that because time is scarce and "there's a sea of new stuff," they would rather invest in reading new comics. Even with them, however, there was a connection between rereading and quality. Daniel hoped to have time in the future to read his "most highly regarded" comics, works like *The Photographer* (2009). Similarly to non-rereaders, Marian, who is a rereader, also mentioned lack of time as a barrier for rereading certain works like *The Sandman* (1991–1997). Since she is now acquainted with the complexity of the work, she "would need to be sure that I have some time to devote to it," showing consequently a considerable level of respect for the work and time that should be devoted to the reading experience. Although maybe optional with other media, rereading is an activity that many of the participants considered crucial and almost intrinsic to comics. Baa defined rereading as constitutive of the comics reading process. For him, most comics "were made to be read more than once due to the amount of things you can absorb and perceive as you keep on looking." Lorraine said, "you['ve] got to reread" because "you read it differently every time!" She does not rewatch movies, but with comics she believes that after one reading, it is difficult to fully appreciate a work and time is necessary to process it adequately. Baa and Lorraine supported the presence of a process of discovery in the action of rereading. For them, it is less about repeating a feeling experienced already but about the certainty that if the first encounter was good, the nature of the medium will make a second encounter still good but different. In her article about the experience of rereading, Hunsberger (1985) describes a similar quality. Referring to Iser, she points to the idea that the text itself has to be rich enough to sustain a second reading experience (p. 162). This quality then connects comics rereading with the medium complexity that participants highlighted at the beginning of this section. The need to reread can also be considered a subjective factor to measure quality. For example, Marian based her purchasing decisions on the potential a text has for rereading. Baa went even further and declared that the desire to reread is crucial in deciding if he has enjoyed a particular comic. He expressed this clearly when he said that "I measure if I really like something or if it really touches me on the [number] of times that I want to see it again."

Hunsberger also indicates that, especially with beginner readers, rereading might be "just a pleasure" (1985, p. 163). This idea can also be expanded and connected to activities of meaning making. For instance, Kalo first connected the act of rereading to the repetition of a pleasurable experience. However, with comics that she described as the "good stuff," this process also offers the possibility of discovering even more richness and depth. Therefore we can strongly connect the processes of exploring meaning and enjoying pleasure. Kalo tends to know by the end of a comic if the work needs to be read again. In some cases, she encounters comics that basically need to be reread because of their density; she gave the autobiographical work of Harvey Pekar as an example, where the art of Robert Crump combined with Pekar's heavy and sarcastic writing usually demand slow reading or rereading. Shade talked similarly about how intricate comics, like *The Invisibles* (1996–2001), benefit from a second reading where "[I] really opened my eyes to all the concepts and story elements that I missed the first time." Again, rereading becomes an activity that reinforces meaning-making processes at the same time as enjoyment.

Jacob revealed another potentially interesting perspective about the theme of rereading. He differentiated a work like *Scott Pilgrim* (2004–2010) that he had purchased because he expects to reread it, from adaptations like

Coraline (2008) or the *Wonderful Wizard of Oz* (2009) that he believes he would not reread. His explanation about rereading *Scott Pilgrim* is similar to other participants' comments: "it just has lots of stuff that you don't notice the first time reading it through, lots of little jokes that are just passing you by cause you're so immersed in the story." Adaptations are a type of text that he often prefers and he explains this preference in these terms:

> You already have an idea of what the story is going be like, so
> I like that because in a way it can almost be more surprising than
> a new story because sometimes new stories can be boring, but
> I think when you have a graphic novel that it's an adaptation
> [and] people can do something that really surprises you.

Although he says that he does not reread adaptations, adaptations in themselves are rereadings. Jacob's explanation about why he enjoys adaptations connects to a process of discovery: looking for missing details or differences that a rich work offers. When one reads adaptation, one might expect a certain amount of fidelity, a connection with the narrative one already knows. Still Jacob says that there is also an element of surprise and novelty. Interesting, then, Jacob's practices are consistent with one of the three perspectives that Hutcheon presents to approach the study of adaptations: "we experience adaptations *(as adaptations)* as palimpsests through our memory of other works that resonate through repetition with variation" (2013, p. 8). Finally, in her conclusion Hunsberger finds "the essence of re-reading" in the activities of interaction and sharing:

> The reader interacts with the text and through it with the author
> in the pursuit of further questions and answers and of a familiar
> and secure world in which to dwell. Sharing also occurs

> between readers who seek, through continued dialogue with each other and the text, a mutual interpretation of the text so that they may establish a shared world ... Thus, while one aspect of the re-reading activity is done alone, re-reading very fundamentally involves engagement with both author and other readers – two differing but vital kinds of interaction and sharing. (1985, p. 166)

I find the idea of considering rereading as social reading very compelling and attractive. However, few of my participants connected rereading with sharing, neither with authors nor with other readers. As I have mentioned, when readers reread, they are looking to deepen their understanding of or their control over the text. Perhaps these readers reread not to encounter the author or other readers, but to encounter their own readings again in the text, thus deepening their understanding of the text and, potentially in the process, their self-understanding as comics readers.

In regards to the concept of satisfaction, I need to focus on Marian since she was the participant who connected this concept more strongly to a good reading experience. Again, identifying the different factors that make a reading material satisfactory was not a straightforward task. She tentatively pointed at the following characteristics to define a satisfactory reading experience:

> Well, it would have a story that's very, that would resonate with me, that would be either very emotionally compelling or really moving in some way. It's like any book, right? The kind of book where you close it and you keep thinking about it for days or weeks or months afterward and it really sticks with you.

As examples, she offered some relatively disparate titles: *Blankets* by Craig Thompson (2003), especially because of its involving story; the manga *Akira* by Katsuhiro Otomo (2000–2002) that she defines as a "rollercoaster"; and the Québécois series *Paul* by Michel Rabagliati (2000–) or the *bande dessinée Ordinary Victories* by Manu Larcenet (2005) both narratives that provoked an unexpected emotional impact. The elements that Marian highlighted in these titles quickly link her thoughts with what Balling also notes in connection with a good reading experience: "[it] is not just about the feelings and emotions the reader experiences during reading; it is also about how the reader experiences the book as an aesthetic and literary object" (2016, p. 45). Marian discussed more concrete aspects of these initial elements in our conversation; it is salient to note that she stayed focused on the works – she did not connect a satisfactory experience to any external factor or situation but just to elements of the work she was reading and what they provoke in her:

- Plotline and textual content: "[*The Sandman*] was really rewarding to read because you never knew what was around the corner and it was well thought [out] and well written."
- Art: Art is what attracts her to a particular title. But "you can have the best art ever, but if you don't have a good story, then it's worthless and probably I'll stop reading."
- Emotion: Something that resonates, that stays with her, that surprises her, a balanced experience that mixes merely entertaining with some careful reflection.
- Length: She expressed a preference for comics that are heavier on text or that create a detailed narrative. For example, she said that "a manga volume . . . would take an hour to read, and then . . . I have to find another soon or otherwise I'll forget what was happening or I'll just waste an hour. I don't know. [Pointing at *Unwritten*] This one has more text in it. A trade is kind

of . . . worthy . . . not worthy, but I just find that there's . . . more satisfaction." She gives *Blankets* and *Akira* both as examples of complex and intricate texts.

These elements helped Marian to describe what she looks for in a satisfactory reading experience: works that were carefully written and plotted, with rather personal artwork and either large, dense graphic novels or serialized works. One can say that they are not surprising but, most important, these elements can be easily connected with the ones Balling mentions when she reports on how her participants articulate a good reading experience (2016, p. 44):

- gain knowledge about the world and oneself
- experience recognition and identification with the characters
- become emotionally involved
- forget time and place
- enjoy a book that is well written
- activate the reader's imagination.

This strong connection with Balling's research creates a bridge between reading experiences, independently of the medium, and demonstrates the richness of comics as reading materials for those who might not yet be convinced of it.

In her focus groups with teenagers, Snowball encountered some participants who disliked graphic novels and declared they did not want to read them (2005). Evidently, my participants enjoy comics, but that enjoyment is not unconditional and they were able to share some unsatisfying reading experiences. Note that most of them are aware of the criticisms and controversies around the medium so they shared a strong discourse in favor of this reading material, but their thoughts about these experiences also show a considerable knowledge about the form and deep care for their relationship with it. Boredom was a sentiment that participants mentioned recurrently to describe unsuccessful reading experiences. Some of the titles that participants mentioned as unsatisfying were relatively surprising. For example, Preacher described such a reading experience as one where "you get too bored" and used his several attempts to read *The Sandman* (1991–1997) as an example. This title has become part of the official canon and because of that Preacher decided to give it a chance. However, the experience was not a good one, as he said that "the beginning didn't grip me and I lost all motivation to keep reading … The artwork was a little weird as well." Because of its status he did not reject the title completely, saying that he might give it another chance eventually. Alison connected boredom to the character of Superman, one of the protagonists in *Trinity* (2009). She describes the character as "boring, really pro America and [not] a very complex character," especially in comparison to Batman. Interesting, she did not completely blame the comic and also pointed to her ignorance about superheroes as something that might have reduced the attractiveness of the title. Alison, along with Kalo and Selina, had strong reactions to *Y: The Last Man* (2003–2008) showcasing the complexity of the reading experience when stories are long and serialized. Selina qualified it as "problematic," but she still read the entire series and declared she liked it. However, for Alison and Kalo, the experience was notably bad and Alison stopped reading without finishing the first volume and Kalo quit after three trade paperbacks. For both of them, it was a problem of expectations. Alison explained that this comic was an opportunity to describe and examine what a world in survival/reconstruction mode and populated just by women would look like. Brian K. Vaughan's take on this story did not impress her; she compared it to writer John Updike, who usually "is transparently writing about his own fantasy" and concluded by saying that "it just bothered me a lot." Similarly, Kalo was attracted to the premise but soon was bothered by the stereotypes used to represent women. Although Selina managed to enjoy

Y: The Last Man (2003–2008), she drew the line at the representation and treatment of Arseface in *Preacher* (1996–2001). The character has a long story arc in the comic and she could not stand its treatment, finding it "bloody offensive" and saying she would "loath going back to it." Although she recognized the edginess and richness of the series, the cruel treatment of this character makes it impossible for her to tolerate the comic. In these comments, we can see reflected problems of representations, either gender or people differently abled, showing that readers look for something beyond mindless entertainment in comics.

Some readers found common practices among the comics industry negatively influencing their reading experiences. For instance, Shade criticized a common practice in the world of superheroes publishing, especially by DC and Marvel, where titles and characters get revamped and relaunched. His reflective analysis deserves a full quote:

> A bad reading experience would be what Jeff Leob did to the Hulk series. Greg Pak had taken a hold of the series and shunted the Hulk off onto a faraway planet where the series transformed from a "monster in the world" to "a monster on a planet of monsters." He created the Hulk as a gladiator warrior, inspiring the hearts of his fellow slaves to become the king of their planet and went so far as father a child. Shortly after they restarted the Hulk series at number one (with Jeff Leob) and returned the Hulk to his brutish "hiding from society" concept. It was a shame, but at the end of the day the property belongs to Marvel and it's in their best interest to return their properties to an easy-to-access state.

Shade was invested in an approach to this character that he clearly considered innovative and experimental, especially for an experienced reader like him. He recognized that these characters are not simply protagonists in storylines for his consumption, but properties that publishing companies use at their leisure to attract consumers to their franchises. Jacob also reflected on economic and production issues and criticized his experiences with adaptations of materials like Pokémon. Adaptations are an important genre for him, as we see in what follows, but he considers that some titles are often published just because "[publishers] know kids are going to buy these; it's more like a franchise, more than 'we want to make a cool graphic novel,' 'we want to showcase our art,' 'we want to tell a story or retell a story.'" Jacob made a connection between commercial products and lack of singularity and how that negatively influences his reading experience. Although this perspective is not unique to the comics medium, it is meaningful to indicate its presence.

Even though all my participants read comics in their free time, the combination of these diverse accounts indicates that they distinctly do not want their comics reading to be taken lightly. It appears that they are attempting to reconcile the stereotypes around the medium with the diversity and complexity that they find in the form and in their own experiences. They might read to have fun or for a mental break, but that does not immediately indicate that they choose comics or reading experiences that are simple, easy, or light. They construct and understand comics as a form full of possibilities, where alternative stories can be told through a combination of elements that make them unique. They appreciate the medium being used to its full potential, implying a certain knowledge about it. At the same time, this is the medium for pleasure reading because of its accessibility and effectiveness in storytelling.

3.2 Materiality Aspects of Comics Reading

In 2014, ComicsPRO, the association of comics retailers, issued a statement reacting to the purchase of Comixology by Amazon (McDonald, 2014):

> There's always a concern when a huge corporation that shows
> little need to turn a profit tries to convert a niche market into
> a commodity. Fortunately there is a *tactile element* to comics
> that no deep-discounting web entity will ever be able to repli-
> cate. So as long as there continues to be fans for *the real thing*,
> there will be comics and comic book stores. [my italics]

Although this statement was predominantly examined as another example of
the potential consequences of yet another large corporation acquiring
a successful small/independent businesses, I was struck by how the retailers
decided to make materiality, the "tactile element," central to their case and to
equate print comics with "the real thing." The discussion that I present here
about the affordances of reading comics in print emerged directly from my
participants. Shade initiated a conversation about acquiring and reading comics
in digital form, primarily to read on his computer and as an alternative to
out-of-print comics. The conversation started, as often happens, with the
comparison between print and digital reading:

> Actually I got to the point too where I didn't like reading comics
> on my computer, even when it was the only thing that I was doing
> I would prefer to have the book. And even now, if there's a series
> that I can't find, I will try to hunt down and pay more than they're
> really worth just because I don't want to read them in my computer
> screen. I don't really know why I like to have them in front of me
> and read it. I don't know. I just can't stand reading a screen,
> I guess.

Although these first words might indicate that the weakness is in the digital
format, in the end there was something else in the experience of reading

a comics in print that made Shade decide that digital reading was not comparable. He explained as follows:

> The fact that these things [comics] contain ideas, this is the closest thing you're going to get to holding an idea, this is the closest thing an idea is gonna become to being physical.

The role of digital devices (in Shade's case represented by the screen) becomes a point of reference to explore and express thoughts about reading in print, breaking through conversations anchored in the dichotomy of the print book versus the digital device. The role and affordances of the material object in the reading experience was the real theme in these discussions. Shade's struggle to express why he gave more value to the print form was not uncommon, and when I asked other participants about their opinions about reading in print or digitally, they generally expressed difficulties in saying exactly why they found reading in print more rewarding. However, this effort turned out to be richly rewarding and eye opening. If reading a comic in print is "the closest thing you're going to get to holding an idea," what other pleasurable, sensorial, and affective experiences do readers connect to this often daily act? Readers want to be transported, immersed in the story, but what other connections do they create during the reading event, and how are these different when the object in hand is in print? Finally, I do not imply in this exploration that content does not matter, or that perhaps in a (close) future we will establish similar connections with digital devices, but I want to invite researchers to reflect beyond content or the dichotomy of print versus digital reading and look at what readers still find significant in reading in print in a heavily digitized society.

The acceptance and integration of digital devices as platforms for reading and consequently the manifestation of new and different ways of reading creates the opportunity to revisit the experience of reading in print. A basic question emerges, for example, when publishers and researchers see that readers still read and purchase books in print even though e-readers are marketed as more efficient and convenient (Sena, 2012). For history of the book scholars, this opportunity is not a surprise since "there is no text apart from the physical support that it offers for its reading (or hearing), hence there is no comprehension of any written piece that does not at least in part depend upon the forms in which it reaches its reader" (Chartier, 1994, p. 9). Books-as-objects also occupy a relevant place in Csikszentmihalyi and Rochberg-Halton's study (1981) about household objects and the feelings that these households' inhabitants developed toward them. Among many other objects, books "are special to people because they serve to embody ideals and to express religious and professional values" (Csikszentmihalyi & Rochberg-Halton, 1981, p. 71). The emergence of digital reading offers a contrasting landscape for researchers to use, but also a new experience for readers who can compare against, struggle with, and seek to define. I am not the first to see this opportunity. In the introduction to a special issue of the *Michigan Review Quarterly* about the future of reading, books, and publishing, Jonathan Freedman noted that beyond discussing, yet again the death of print, "we might also be present at the birth of the bookish, the reassertion and reimagination of the constellation of values and meanings traditionally associated with 'the book'" (Freedman, 2009). However, researchers seem more engaged with discovering how reading is changed by the digital format, often comparing print and digital platforms and devices. Considering this material aspect in relation to comics reading is even more pertinent because of the success of digital platforms such as *Comixology* and also because of the consequences of this success.

The study of reading in print and reading digitally has blossomed in the past ten years. Mainly two approaches are used to explain the differences between reading in these two media: the cognitive approach and the medium materiality approach (see Hou, Rashid, & Lee, 2017 for a more extensive analysis of these approaches). As I have mentioned before, the present discussion is connected to recent calls from scholars for a multidimensional approach to the study of reading, and this section, inevitably, tries to expand upon these two approaches. In relation to comics studies, this section connects to recent interest from scholars who have acknowledged the importance of materiality in comics production and analysis (Kashtan, 2013), carried out projects where comics are studied from the perspective of the five senses (Hague, 2014) and examined material aspects in the works of alternative comics creators (Tinker, 2007).

The discussion around reading and technology is often fittingly presented in binary terms: to use or not to use. As Tveit and Mangen note, a common response to the preference for paper instead of digital devices is that of habit (2014, p. 183), an inclination that is also frequently coupled with Luddite or technophobic affinities. This dichotomy needs to be complicated, and my participants' reflections alongside other research examples postulate a situated examination of reading and technology, thus substituting the binary approach for a richer and more complex spectrum. Rouncefield and Tolmie's research (2011) helps to clarify what I try to encapsulate in this idea of the spectrum. They examine how reading is part of daily routines, especially in the home, and how these routines might affect the adoption of e-readers or the continued use of print books. One of their main conclusions supports the idea that one new technology does not simply replace the old one, but that individuals assess the affordances that each technology offers and choose them for particular times. This evolutionary instead of revolutionary approach strengthens the importance of looking at technology in context and from the perspective of its users. Even more relevant for these discussions is how the authors highlight the fact that "reading is not just a matter of consuming words off the page" but also an activity connected to the accomplishment of other activities, and I would add mental or emotional states: "'relaxing,' 'killing time,' 'informing,' 'having a break,' 'putting to bed,' and so on" (p. 138). Similarly, Hupfeld, Sellen, O'Hara, & Rodden (2013) also advocate for avoiding the study of new reading devices in isolation but as part of a larger ecosystem that more often than not includes print books (p. 5). Although their study is indeed focused on e-reading, its implications affect print books, since readers' general practices are altered, complemented, and augmented by these devices (p. 15). Again, similarly to Rouncefield and Tomie's study, the researchers detected that people's practices and orientations surrounding e-books shifted in emphasis from the book as artifact to a set of activities or experiences associated with reading (p. 17). Interesting, their conclusions also supported the idea that the competitive environment created between print and digital reading is one created by corporate interests that understand attention as economic profit.

The words of my participants revealed that they have also internalized the discourse about using print and digital devices as a dichotomy instead of a spectrum. For example, Templesmith explained, "I don't say by any means that I'm against technology because I play a lot of videogames too, but I don't know, it's not the same." They recurrently mentioned playing videogames as a proof of their comfort with technology, and several participants (Oracle, Demi, Kalo, HunterS, and Shalmanaser) described themselves as active videogame players. They similarly referred to having owned or not being opposed to owning an e-reading device and were aware of and recognized the potential benefits that their use could have. Shade shared his support for e-readers and tablets when he pointed to their potentially integral role for readers who live in areas without access to bookstores or comics stores. Participants acknowledged the convenience of e-readers and tablets, especially for storage and transportation, as well as the possibilities of connectivity and multitasking. However, they also admitted that the reading experience would change. Anecdotally, in her research, Tinker makes a similar comparison with the two works that she studies: "it is hard to imagine reading *Jimmy Corrigan* or *Blankets* entirely from a screen" (2007, p. 1180). This thought resonates with a comment from Baa, one of the participants who used an iPad and some apps for comics reading. He admitted that these platforms would not work for all comics: "I downloaded the *Marvel* app and I really like it, but imagine reading *Watchmen* or something like that; it wouldn't work."

Reading comics in digital environments can happen on computers, e-readers, or other mobile devices, and any of these devices often provide the possibility of connectivity and multitasking. The choice of print then becomes the choice of disconnecting, of isolating ourselves. When these readers chose print materials, it was in many cases because they were seeking isolation and concentration. For example, Alison commented on how while reading on the computer she feels tempted to do fact checking and multitask: "I don't like being on the computer very much and I get distracted if I'm reading it on the computer; I'll open up other tabs and do other things[and] I just think that when I'm on the computer, I feel like I need to be clicking things all the time or something." Devi expressed a similar worry because she "can't focus as easily on the art and become[s] easily distracted by other things on [her] computer." Again, this need for disconnecting is not unique, and one of the participants in media scholar Ytre-Arne's research about women's magazine reading (2011a, 2011b) eloquently explained that her preference for print magazines is based on the fact that she likes that "the picture in front of me is quiet" (2011a, p. 471). Therefore, it is essential to highlight that print is chosen because of its intrinsic limitations that suddenly become considerable advantages. These advantages can be easily contextualized in terms of a general pushback to find quiet times away from technology (e.g., Foot, 2014; Morrison & Gomez, 2014), technology resistance (Bauer, 1998), or the problematization of the idea of the digital divide (e.g., Reisdorf, Axelsson, & Söderholm, 2012; Selwyn, 2006, 2003).

The discourses of technophobia, technophilia, or print nostalgia polarize and compartmentalize the potential explanations that reflect complex and rich behaviors resulting from a complex media ecology. The objective should be to look for ways to research the coexistence of both reading materials, the experiences and practices emerging from this coexistence, and the labor that readers perform to select texts, moments, and spaces that are adequate for each.

At this point it is relevant to return to a discussion of Shade's quote since it is at the core of this section's analysis. Shade praised the fact that reading print comics is "the closest thing you're going to get to holding an idea." The use of the verb "hold" and the notion of the potential "physicality" of an idea mark the importance of reflecting about sensorial aspects in the reading experience, an activity that is primarily researched as an intellectual, cognitive, intangible experience. Going back to Ytre-Arne's project on women readers and magazines, she reports the use of a similar sentence, "you can hold [it] in your hands," when participants tried to explore the differences between reading print magazines and their online version (2011b, p. 471). She also highlights a similar difficulty that participants experienced to explain the importance of this characteristic, where "most informants used general phrases like 'it feels different' or 'it's more special'" (Ytre-Arne, 2011b, pp. 471–472). My participants shared that struggle, but I believe that in this struggle there is something worth our attention and study. I want to consider my participants' comments thoughtful and descriptive reflections about their experiences. Shade was not alone in sharing ideas about the importance of the materiality when reading in print. Kalo spoke of the uniqueness of "picking up a book"; Templesmith talked about enjoying "holding a book, and smelling it"; Preacher said that "nothing compares to actually holding the story in your hand." Some of them turned to certain shared and recurrent comments about the smell or touch of the print comic, but even the repetition of these depictions helps to establish their importance. Moreover, comments such as those from Preacher or Shade explore relevant ideas about the embodiment of the reading experience and the importance of print comics for such embodiment. This embodiment and the materiality of print comics are expressed and appreciated in different ways by different participants. In 2002, Ruecker reported on a project to study how to successfully design an e-book. The summary of what their participants liked will sound familiar, almost repetitive:

> Physically, they liked the fact that books are static and quiet. They liked the smell, feel and shape, and enjoyed holding books while reading. Some respondents enjoyed turning pages, the feel of paper, while others enjoyed marking their books. (2002, p. 135)

Although other factors such as the cultural and symbolic capital of print books as well as their collecting and displaying value were mentioned, Ruecker's (2002) main objective was trying to harness the pleasurable experience here described by readers to an e-book. It is not surprising that the concept of pleasure is of interest for designers, since when usability is at the center of the design process, people are simply thought of as users. However, the introduction of pleasure moves the discussion to people's "hopes, fears, dreams, aspirations, tastes and personality" (Jordan, 2002, p. 377). One of the main changes that pleasure-based approaches bring to product design is a holistic conceptualization of people, "as rational, emotional and hedonistic beings," and advocates for the design of products "as living-objects with which people have relationships" (Jordan, 2006). Notions of pleasure were implicit in the conversations with my participants not only since our conversations were focused on reading for pleasure, but pleasure was also primary in their use of sensorial and affective terms to describe their preference for print comics.

Kalo, Marian, and Daniel explored almost expertly the idea of comics-as-objects. Discussing considerations about quality in relation to both content and container when purchasing comics, Kalo expressed a strong preference for works published by Drawn & Quarterly (D&Q) because she "feel[s] that they really care about quality." Daniel described D&Q as a "close second" to his favorite publisher, Fantagraphics, and D&Q's status was mostly motivated by the material quality of its comics production. The visual component of the comics language makes these material aspects extremely important and influential in the reading experience. As much as creators, as Tinker (2007) points out, are aware of and careful about them, readers will also be devoted to publishers that are thoughtful about the size of the book, the type and finish of the paper, the ink/color quality, the binding quality, etc. For example, Marian speaks of this conceptualization of comics as "art objects," and the meaning that a physical work has for her: "sometimes I'll buy a book and it's just, it's almost as much for the story as it is for 'I want that object,' I just think it's really neat, it's like having a piece of art on your wall in a way." The comic does not become just any object, but an art object for her, and this approach clearly explains, for example, why she would acquire free webcomics in print format.[4]

Enriching this discussion about comics-as-objects, Baa focused the conversation even more on the issue of paper: "there are different kinds of paper, so I guess that if I read on an e-book, I just don't get the same quality of ... maybe with time, it could but ... there's certain kinds of papers that are really good to read [on]." In his multisensorial exploration of comics, Hague carefully examines the tactile properties of comics: texture

---

[4] Beaty (2012) expands on the discussion about comics as art object from a literary and aesthetic perspective, especially about issues related to the presence of comics in museum or boundaries between highbrow and lowbrow culture and works.

(e.g., thickness and gloss of paper), compositing materials, hardness, flexibility, or weight (2014, p. 99). Although Baa was the only participant who referred to paper as an element to consider, his comment allows me to bring into the discussion the work of designer Ken'ya Hara, whose words are thought-provoking in relation not just to print comics but also to book printing and its future:

> Thanks to the rise of electronic media, paper can finally behave as it can and should – as an intrinsically charming material. If electronic media [are] reckoned a practical tool for information conveyance, books are information sculpture; from now on, books will probably be judged according to how well they awaken this materiality, because the decision to create a book at all will be based on a definite choice of paper as the medium. How fortunate an issue this will be for paper. (Hara, 2007, p. 201)

Hara's description of electronic media as a "practical tool" connects directly with previous quotes from my participants describing the differences between digital and print reading materials. Moreover, Hara connects the future success of books to "how well they awaken this materiality," and he describes paper as "an intrinsically charming material." Hara might be a bit hyperbolic in his discussion, but his depiction of paper as "charming" acknowledges the presence of a viewer/reader who needs to be charmed, attracted, or fascinated by the experience of touching, holding, and even reading the book. I do not deny that his words could be characterized as perfectly fitting in the discourse of *print nostalgia*. Nevertheless, this rather extreme position helps to accentuate the importance of a turn to the material as a contrast to the omnipresent digital.

In order to explain and share the singularity of print reading, participants often struggled to examine the reading experience as a phenomenon with boundaries and specific characteristics, then digital reading often became a backdrop for comparison. Baa told us, "when you are reading digitally, the reader [reading device] has to be really good for you to get this experience." What is the experience he is referring to? He previously described it as follows: "you go back and forth so you can look at the little images, the bigger picture, the way the borders are set; you can get something from it." He connects print to a kinetic and visual experience, to the careful observation and absorption of comics art. The uniqueness of comics at communicating through text and image is especially important. Art tends to provoke a more immediate reaction, what Goldsmith calls the "visceral pull" in her explanation of the difference between readers' advisory with graphic novels and with other books (2010, p. 6). Devi also focused on this visual component of comics when she said, "the art is different when it's on a page than when it's online . . . Not actually different but it feels different." Commenting on this difference from the production side, Daniel concluded that "anything analog versus digital, there's always people [who] prefer one over the other. I'm a mixed bag; digital is easier, it's more efficient, it's faster . . . but it produces a different look, different sound, different feel." Like Hara, Daniel also used terminology related to convenience to describe digital production and insisted on the idea of a different sensorial experience. Some ideas from Phil Jones, a design scholar, serve to keep building on the different aspects to explore in print comics. Jones introduces a new framework to understand material and meaning-making in aspects of book design and concludes his literature review about materialism and dematerialism in book design with the following thought:

> Accordingly the book designer's task becomes one of synchro-
> nizing the different elements of the book, to achieve a unity,

a "pervasive quality" or "atmosphere." A quality that is affective while sympathetic to the text and the act of reading by not compromising on issues of readability and legibility. (Jones, 2011, p. 262)

The use of terms like "atmosphere," "unity," and "pervasive quality" to describe the balance that book design should achieve clearly seeks to harness similar qualities as those described by my participants. Jones also mentioned the idea of being "affective," perhaps another way of referring to what Hara described as "charming," since in the end it acknowledges the presence of a reader with aesthetic and sensorial needs. This quote summarizes a moment, an event, when a reader holds a book to be immersed in the narrative (readability and legibility), but part of the moment is also created/supported by the material qualities transmitted through the materiality and design. In this reading event, readability and legibility are key, but the effort to create a seamless but, most important, sensorial, even possibly affective experience between text and reader should not be ignored.

"For books that matter, people choose printed books" (Hupfeld et al., 2013, p. 15). Hupfeld and her colleagues summarized with this sentence one of their main conclusions. Up to this point, I have looked at how print comics offer moments of silence and how they are constructed as (art) objects enjoyed for their physical/aesthetic qualities. I am now immersing you into an examination of the reading moment and how my participants – and as I have presented others before – described the different reading experience facilitated by print materials, one that can be constructed as whole, easier to remember and to make part of one's personal narrative.

My participants found that reading in print has a different "feel." Design scholar Phil Jones considers the use of "feel" significant in his own research because it "introduces emotion into an account of the experiencing of a book"

(2011, p. 262). To explore the importance of this verb, Jones briefly brings into the discussion the work of philosopher Mark Johnson and the concept of *flow of experience*, explained as "unified wholes (gestalts) that are pervaded by an all-encompassing quality that makes the present situation what and how it is" (2007, p. 73). From my project, there is another quality of the *flow of experience* that is more relevant and will potentially help the unpacking of expressions such as the "whole experience." Based on Dewey, Johnson explores the idea that "[a]n identifiable, meaningful experience is neither merely emotional, nor merely practical, nor merely intellectual. Rather, it is all of these at once and together" (p. 74). This effort to bring emotion, practice, and intellect into the full experience of reading highlights the importance of the recurrent use of the verb *feel* to explain the experience of looking at the art of print comics or simply reading in print. For these readers, reading a print comic *feels* like a whole experience "pervaded by unifying qualities that demarcate them within the flux of our lives" (Johnson, 2007, p. 75). It is important to try to examine these "unifying qualities," and here Shade again illuminates this point when he explains how he enjoys "[t]he paper, the book, the whole package of it in one physical thing, I guess I prefer that."

Therefore, as a reader, a print book is "the whole package." If one thinks of reading simply as an informational act, as an event where we "consume words," it is difficult to imagine how embodiment or the physical engagement with a book instead of a digital device would be radically distinct. However, if one thinks of reading as an event that potentially produces meaning beyond what is in the text, but meaning in the life of the reader, in her history as a reader, in her personal development as a reader, the situatedness of the experience and the confluence of content and container in one (the book) in the hands of other (the reader) will potentially matter. When Shade is reading a print comic, container and content are one. This is something very different than reading on a tablet or e-reader, where the container stays the same for different narratives, even different activities. Johnson's explanation speaks to the importance of the print material in a reading experience during the reading event. However, there is another potential context where the collapse of content and container become relevant, memory and remembering.

In *Evocative Objects*, Turkle explores the role of objects as "companions to our emotional lives or as provocations to thought" (2007, p. 5). The idea of print books as "companions" is recurrent in explanations about the preference for print. But how does this companionship develop? Why and how can a cheap paperback of Harry Potter become important for an adult reader? Intuitively, we can offer explanations about emotional attachment, nostalgia, or reminiscence. Although I am not negating the possibility that we will develop similar attachments to digital devices, is there any potential explanation to the efficiency of print books in this role? Researching memory and retrieval, Morineau, Blanche, Tobin, and Guéguen explore the ability of the e-book versus the paper book as an "external memory trigger" (2005, p. 329), as a "contextual index for the retrieval of encoded information" (p. 334). The researchers identify the ability of the device to hold multiple contents as problematic to fulfill this memory-related work; again one of the main affordances of the digital platform becomes problematic. They conclude that "it does not provide the external indicators to memory that the classical book does, in that it does not serve as an unambiguous index to indicate a field of knowledge on the basis of its particular physical form" (p. 346). The idea of the book as a contextual index can be expanded beyond serving as a contextual index for information in itself but also to serve as an index for one's reader self-development and history: one reader, one context, one narrative, and one book can help make one experience whole and identifiable. Kalo offered another layer to this discussion. She talked about herself as a collector of both books and comics. However, she does not preserve them in mint condition, as she said, "they are in my condition": she writes on them, marks them, and rereads them.

In this process she creates traces of herself and her reader-self that can be preserved and revisited. From these traces emerges the role of print reading material as an index in the story of the reader-self. Finally, this conceptualization of books materiality potentially brings a rich theoretical framework to a common explanation for the preference of print books.

The physicality of comics, and by extension other reading materials, should remain central to research and questions about their reception and consequently about their place in personal and library collections. The matter of this discussion has not been if reading in print is better or worse, more effective or less effective than reading in digital form. Instead, my participants have helped us to explore ideas about how the change of media can potentially change our relationship to reading and our relationship to the reading material. More specifically, from their struggle to explain the importance of print comics emerges a rich discourse about the importance of materiality in the reading experience: how print weaknesses create moments of retreat for readers in connected world, how material qualities emphasize the aesthetic pleasure of reading (and owning a comics), and how the singularity in the print reading experience creates marks in their personal stories. This project also reinforces the importance of talking to real readers and draws commonalities between projects from different fields that bring these voices to the discussion. The idea of reading as a situated practice also appears important for LIS scholars and practitioners, since this research hopefully helps to show that privileging one format without knowing the community preferences and routines might be a fatal mistake. I do not deny the possibility that in the future, readers may develop relationships to reading devices in ways similar to what is currently happening with cellphones or computers (Beer, 2012). However, each of those relationships deserves exploration in its own way and more research projects should also examine their cohabitation in everyday life, beyond the competitive discourse for attention.

4 The Comics Reading Experience: Beyond Denigration, Instrumentality, and Complacency

Reading is an elusive practice. Rothbauer (2009), for example, speaks about the placelessness of reading among rural teens. In my writing, I have discussed the transient, almost invisible, nature of being a comics reader, especially a female reader. The experience of comics reading can occur through different formats, at different moments in life, and for different purposes; however, this rich and chameleonic practice has long been *invisible* because the experience itself was neglected or undervalued. In other cases, this reading experience was subsumed under the fan experience and was therefore not recognized as a distinctive practice that could be something different than being a fan. In contrast with this elusiveness of the reading experience, in publishing, young adult literature and comics are achieving a degree of recognition and success, with increasing mainstream visibility and scholarly recognition. I feel privileged to have worked with these readers; their engagement and expertise reveals them to be conscientious and reflexive readers who, either as beginners or experts, show a serious commitment to the medium. My call is for comics readers and comics reading to receive some deserved attention and respect because this project demonstrates the meaningful contributions that the experiences of comics readers can make to both reading studies and comics research, as well as help educators and librarians understanding the factors that contribute to the importance of comics reading in the lives of many young people.

Considering comics reading among the many media practices of youth is essential, particularly when one sees the seamless and fundamental role that comics reading occupies as part of their identities and lives. Historically, the expectation was that if you are committed to read comics, inevitably you are, will become, or are expected to become a fan. These readers share the difficulty to define one's relationship to a certain type of media and in the process of unpacking this, they reveal this relationship as mutable and multifaceted since taste, engagement, and commitment can change under many different circumstances. Prevalent stereotypes of comics reading as light or easy reading and of comics readers as readers who lack some reading skill are challenged, thus the comics reading experience becomes something else than transient, trivial, or a crutch for reluctant readers. More important, comics reading emerges as a practice that adapts to youth's lives, and comics readers do not need to "grow out of" comics and move to better or more text-focused reading materials, but they "grow with" comics. Recent events such as the expansion of Gamergate to the realm of comics, Comicsgate (Proctor & Kies, 2018), exemplify the importance of continuing the exploration of gender issues and belonging among and in the comics community. In this project, female participants brought these issues to the forefront and shared their struggle to become a recognized part of the culture and also to change it to create their own space in it. The visibility of female readers and their multiple roles as readers, reading mentors, creators, fans, and comics store owners demonstrate that they also deserve to be at the center of studying comics reading and the comics community.

Comics reading emerges as a sophisticated practice that shares elements with other media practices but that also has unique characteristics that make it especially suitable for and compatible with some of the conditions young people live under in contemporary society. These participants describe a complex medium that challenges and comforts them, that is accessible but is also intricate and that deserves time and attention; it is one that is unique but that also easily becomes part of their individual and communal media landscape. This landscape creates more possibilities for readers to experience the text, to create meaning and memories, and for scholars to study why and how each technology and narrative is integrated and experienced.

All these different elements portray a sophisticated relationship between readers and their comics that should also be of interest for librarians and educators for two key reasons: first, it supports the presence and the integration of comics in library collections and programming as well as part of educational curricula; and second, if comics and the reading experience can be described with this level of subtlety and richness, can we consequently begin looking at comics readers also as sophisticated and multifaceted readers?

These readers showcase the difficulty of defining one's relationship to a certain type of media, a struggle that should spark our curiosity as researchers when we inhabit a media landscape saturated by a multiplicity of media technologies and narratives. The experiences that emerge from this project help to characterize young adults as readers who have busy lives and are strategic about their reading selections; for many of them, their reading agendas are still packed with compulsory materials from school, thus their reading for pleasure choices vary tremendously, from challenging and complex readings to satisfying and enjoyable texts, and in some cases, comics are the reading materials that combine both.

References

Alverson, B. (October 2017). NYCC Insider Sessions Powered by ICv2: A Demographic Snapshot of Comics Buyers. ICv2. Available at: https://icv2.com/articles/news/view/38709/nycc-insider-sessions-powered-icv2-a-demographic-snapshot-comics-buyers (accessed October 15, 2018).

Amalgam. (2018). About Us. Available at: www.amalgamphilly.com/whatthe frak/ (accessed October 15, 2018).

Arizpe, E. & Cliff Hodges, G. (eds.) (2018). *Young People Reading: Empirical Research across International Contexts*. London, UK: Routledge.

Balling, G. (2016). What Is a Reading Experience? The Development of a Theoretical and Empirical Understanding. In P. Rothbauer, K. I. Skjerdingstad, L. McKechnie, & K. Oterholm (eds.), *Plotting the Reading Experience: Theory, Practice, Politics*. Waterloo, ON: Wilfrid Laurier University Press, pp. 37–53.

Bauer, M. (1998). *Resistance to New Technology: Nuclear Power, Information Technology and Biotechnology*. Cambridge, UK: Cambridge University Press.

Beaty, B. (2012). *Comics versus Art: Comics in the Art World*. Toronto, ON: University of Toronto Press.

Beer, D. (2012). The Comfort of Mobile Media: Uncovering Personal Attachments with Everyday Devices. *Convergence: The International Journal of Research into New Media Technologies* 18 (4), 361–367.

Botzakis, S. (2011a). "To Be a Part of the Dialogue": American Adults Reading Comic Books. *Journal of Graphic Novels and Comics* 2 (2), 113–123.

    (2011b). Becoming Life-Long Readers: Insights from a Comics Book Reader. In D. E. Alvermann & K. A. Hinchman (eds.),

References

Reconceptualizing the Literacies in Adolescent's Lives: Bridging the Everyday/Academic Divide. New York, NY: Routledge, pp. 29–48.

   (2009). Adult Fans of Comic Books: What They Get Out of Reading. *Journal of Adolescent & Adult Literacy* 53 (1), 50–59.

Botzakis, S., Savitz, R., & Low, D. E. (2017). Adolescents Reading Graphic Novels and Comics: What We Know from Research. In K. A. Hinchman & D. A. Appleman (eds.), *Adolescent Literacies: A Handbook of Practice-Based Research*. New York, NY: Guilford Publications, pp. 310–322.

Brown, J. A. (2001). *Black Superheroes, Milestone Comics, and Their Fans*. Jackson, MI: University Press of Mississippi.

Budd, J. M. (1995). An Epistemological Foundation for Library and Information Science. *Library Quarterly* 65 (3), 295–318.

Busse, K. (2013). Geek Hierarchies, Boundary Policing, and the Gendering of the Good Fan.*Participations* 10 (1), 73–91. Available at: www.participations.org/Volume%2010/Issue%201/6%20Busse%2010.1.pdf (accessed October 15, 2018).

Busse, K. & Gray, J. (2011). Fan Cultures and Fan Communities. In V. Nightingale (ed.), *The Handbook of Media Audiences*. Oxford, UK: Blackwell, pp. 425–443.

Cedeira Serantes, L. (2016). When Comics Set the Pace: The Experience of Time and the Reading of Comics. In L. McKechnie, P. Rothbauer, K. Oterholm, & K. I. Skjerdingstad (eds.), *Plotting the Reading Experience: Theory, Practice, Politics*. Waterloo, ON: Wilfrid Laurier University Press, pp. 217–232.

   (2013). Misfits, Loners, Immature Students, Reluctant Readers: Librarianship Participates in the Construction of Teen Comics Readers. In A. Bernier (ed.), *Transforming Young Adult Services: A Reader for Our Age*. New York, NY: Neal-Schuman, pp. 115–135.

References

(2009). "I'm a Marvel Girl": Exploration of the Selection Practices of Comic Book Readers. In P. Rothbauer, S. Stevenson, & N. Wathen (eds.), *Canadian Association for Information Science Conference: Mapping the 21st Century Information Landscape: Borders, Bridges and Byways*. Available at: dwww.researchgate.net/profile/Lucia_Cedeira_Serantes/publication/242783525_I'm_a_Marvel_girl_Exploration_of_the_Selection_Practices_of_Comic_Book_Readers/links/004635367bfc82b80f000000.p (accessed October 15, 2018).

Chartier, R. (1994). *The Order of Books: Readers, Authors, and Libraries in Europe between the Fourteenth and Eighteenth Centuries*. Stanford, CA: Stanford University Press.

Chute, H. L. & DeKoven, M. (2006). Introduction: Graphic Narrative. *MFS: Modern Fiction Studies* 52 (4), 767–782.

Cliff Hodges, G. (2016). *Researching and Teaching Reading: Developing Pedagogy through Critical Enquiry*. New York, NY: Routledge.

Cohen, M. Z., Kahn, D. L., & Steeves, R. H. (2000). *Hermeneutic Phenomenological Research: A Practical Guide for Nurse Researchers*. Thousand Oaks, CA; London, UK; New Delhi, India: Sage.

Collinson, I. (2009). *Everyday Readers: Reading and Popular Culture*. London, UK: Equinox.

Comic Book League Defense Fund. (2018a). Case Study: Persepolis. Available at: http://cbldf.org/banned-challenged-comics/case-study-persepolis// (accessed March 15, 2018).

(2018b). Case Study: Fun Home. Available at: http://cbldf.org/banned-challenged-comics/case-study-fun-home// (accessed March 15, 2018).

Csikszentmihalyi, M. & Rochberg-Halton, E. (1981). Books. In *The Meaning of Things: Domestic Symbols and the Self*. New York, NY: Cambridge University Press, pp. 69–71.

References

de Certeau, M. (1984). *The Practice of Everyday Life*. Berkeley, CA: University of California Press.

Delany, S. R. & Groth, G. (1979). An Interview with Samuel R. Delany. *Comics Journal* 48, 36–71.

Ferguson, K., Brown, N., & Piper, L. (2014). "How Much Can One Book Do? Exploring Perceptions of a Common Book Program for First-Year University Students. *Journal of College Reading and Learning* 44 (2), 164–199.

Finlay, L. (2002). "Outing" the Researcher: The Provenance, Process, and Practice of Reflexivity. *Qualitative Health Research* 12 (4), 531–545.

Fiske, J. (1992). The Cultural Economy of Fandom. In L. A. Lewis (ed.), *The Adoring Audience: Fan Culture and Popular Media*. London, UK: Routledge, pp. 30–49.

Foot, K. (2014). The Online Emergence of Pushback on Social Media in the United States: A Historical Discourse Analysis. *International Journal of Communication*, 8, 1313–1342.

Frank, J. (1944). What's in the Comics? *Journal of Educational Sociology*, 18 (4), 214–22.

Freedman, J. (2009). bookishNess: A Brief Introduction. *Michigan Quarterly Review*, 48 (4). Available at: http://hdl.handle.net/2027/spo.act2080.00 48.401 (accessed March, 1 2018).

Fuller, D. & Rehberg Sedo, D. (2013) *Reading beyond the Book: The Social Practices of Contemporary Literary Culture*. New York, NY: Routledge.

Gabilliet, J. (2010). *Of Comics and Men: A Cultural History of American Comic Books*. Jackson, MI: University Press of Mississippi.

Gallik, J. D. (1999). Do They Read for Pleasure? Recreational Reading Habits of College Students. *Journal of Adolescent & Adult Literacy*, 42 (6), 480–488.

References

The Geek Initiative. (2018) Inclusive Comic Book Stores. *thegeekinitiative*. Available at: https://geekinitiative.com/female-friendly-comic-book-stores/ (accessed April 15, 2018).

Gibson, M. (2015). *Remembered Reading: Memory, Comics and Post-War Constructions of British Girlhood*. Leuven: Leuven University Press.

 (2008). What You Read and Where You Read It, How You Get It, How You Keep It: Children, Comics and Historical Cultural Practice. *Popular Narrative Media*, 1 (2), 151–168.

Goldsmith, F. (2017). *The Readers' Advisory Guide to Graphic Novels*, 2nd edn. Chicago, IL: American Library Association.

 (2010). What's in a Name: Nomenclature and Libraries. In R. G. Weiner, ed., *Graphic Novels and Comics in Libraries and Archives: Essays on Readers, Research, History and Cataloging*. Jefferson, NC: McFarland, pp. 185–191.

Hague, I. (2014). *Comics and the Senses: A Multisensory Approach to Comics and Graphic Novels*. New York, NY; London, UK: Routledge.

Hammond, H. (2012). Graphic Novels and Multimodal Literacy: A High School Study with *American Born Chinese*. *Bookbird: A Journal of International Children's Literature*, 50 (4), 22–32.

Hara, K. (2007). Books As Information Sculpture. In K. Hara, ed., *Designing Design*. Baden, Switzerland: Lars Müller Publishers, pp. 196–209.

Hatfield, C. (2005). *Alternative Comics : An Emerging Literature*. Jackson, MS: University of Mississippi Press.

 (2009). An Art of Tensions. In J. Heer & K. Worcester, eds., *Comics Studies Reader*. Jackson, MS: University of Mississippi Press, pp. 132–148.

Hatfield, C. & Svonkin, C. (2012). Why Comics Are and Are Not Picture Books: Introduction. *Children's Literature Association Quarterly*, 37 (4), 429–435.

Heer, J. & Worcester, K. (2009). *A Comics Studies Reader*. Jackson, MI: University Press of Mississippi.

References

Hills, M. (2002). *Fan Cultures*. London; New York, NY: Routledge.

Hou, J., Rashid, J., & Min Lee, K. (2017). Cognitive Map or Medium Materiality? Reading on Paper and Screen. *Computers in Human Behavior*, 67, 84–94.

Howard, V. (2011). The Importance of Pleasure Reading in the Lives of Young Teens: Self-Identification, Self-Construction and Self-Awareness. *Journal of Librarianship and Information Science*, 43 (1), 46–55.

(2009). Peer Group Influences on Avid Teen Readers. *New Review of Children's Literature and Librarianship*, 14 (2), 103–119.

Hughes, J. M., King, A., Perkins, P., & Fuke, V. (2011). Adolescents and "Autographics": Reading and Writing Coming-of-Age Graphic Novels. *Journal of Adolescent & Adult Literacy*, 54 (8), 601–612.

Hughes-Hassell, S. & Rodge, P. (2007). The Leisure Reading Habits of Urban Adolescents. *Journal of Adolescent & Adult Literacy*, 51 (1), 22–33.

Hunsberger, M. (1985). The Experience of Re-reading. *Phenomenology + Pedagogy*, 3 (3), 161–166.

Hupfeld, A., Sellen, A., O'Hara, K., & Rodden, T. (2013). Leisure-Based Reading and the Place of E-Books in Everyday Life. *INTERACT'13*, 1–18.

Hutcheon, L. (2013). *A Theory of Adaptation*. London: Routledge.

Jacobs, D. (2013). *Graphic Encounters: Comics and the Sponsorship of Multimodal Literacy*. New York, NY: Bloomsbury.

Jenkins, H. (1992). *Textual Poachers: Television Fans & Participatory Culture*. New York, NY: Routledge.

Johnson, M. (2007). *The Meaning of the Body*. Chicago, IL: University of Chicago Press.

Johnsson-Smaragdi, U. & Jönsson, A. (2006). Book Reading in Leisure Time: Long-Term Changes in Young Peoples' Book Reading Habits. *Scandinavian Journal of Educational Research*, 50 (5), 519–40.

References

Jones, P. (2011). Looking through, Looking into and Looking at the Book: The Materiality of Message and Medium. *Book 2.0*, 1 (2), 255–271.

Jordan, P. W. (2002). Conclusions. In P. W. Jordan & W. S. Green, eds., *Pleasure with Products: Beyond Usability*. London: Taylor & Francis, pp. 63–64.

(2006). Creating Pleasurable Products. *International Encyclopedia of Ergonomics and Human Factors*, pp. 1095–1097.

Kashtan, A. (2013). My Mother Was a Typewriter: *Fun Home* and the Importance of Materiality in Comics Studies. *Journal of Graphic Novels and Comics*, 4 (1), 92–116.

Kvale, S. & Brinkmann, S. (2009). *InterViews: Learning the Craft of Qualitative Research Interviewing*. Thousand Oaks, CA: Sage.

Lent, J. A. (1999). *Pulps Demons: International Dimensions of the Postwar Anti-Comics Campaign*. Teaneck, NJ: Fairleigh Dickinson University Press.

Long, E. (2003). *Book Clubs: Women and the Uses of Reading in Everyday Life*. Chicago, IL: University of Chicago Press.

Macdonald, H. (June 2017). This Week's BookScan Chart Is a Wake-Up Call for the Comics Industry. *The Beat: The Newsblog of Comics Culture*. Available at: www.comicsbeat.com/this-weeks-bookscan-chart-is-a-wake-up-call-for-the-comics-industry/ (accessed October 15, 2018).

Mackey, M. (2007a). *Literacies across Media: Playing the Text*, 2nd edn. New York, NY: Routledge.

(2007b). *Mapping Recreational Literacies: Contemporary Adults at Play*. New York, NY: Peter Lang.

(2011). *Narrative Pleasures in Young Adult Novels, Films, and Video Games*. Houndmills: Palgrave Macmillan.

Mangen, A. & van der Weel, A. (2016). The Evolution of Reading in the Age of Digitisation: An Integrative Framework for Reading Research. *Literacy*, 50 (3), 116–124.

References

Marston, G. (October 5, 2017). Retailers become heated over Marvel Variants, Diversity in Closed-Doors. *Newsarama*. Available at: www.newsarama.com/36750-retailers-become-heated-over-marvel-variants-diversity-in-closed-doors-nycc-panel.html (accessed on March 1, 2018).

McCloud, S. (1994). *Understanding Comics*. New York, NY: HarperPerennial.

McDonald, H. (2014). ComicsPRO Responds to Comixology/Amazon Deal. Available at: www.comicsbeat.com/comicspro-responds-to-comixologyamazon-deal/ (Accessed March 1, 2018).

McRobbie, A. (1991). *Feminism and Youth Culture: From "Jackie" to "Just Seventeen."* Boston, MA: Unwin Hyman.

Mokhtari, K., Reichard, C. A., & Gardner, A. (2009). The Impact of Internet and Television Use on the Reading Habits and Practices of College Students. *Journal of Adolescent & Adult Literacy*, 52 (7), 609–619.

Morineau, T., Blanche, C., Tobin, L. & Guéguen, N. (2005). The Emergence of the Contextual Role of the E-Book in Cognitive Processes through an Ecological and Functional Analysis. *International Journal of Human–Computer Studies*, 62 (3), 329–348.

Morrison, S. & Gomez, R. (2014). Pushback: Expressions of Resistance to the "Evertime" of Constant Online Connectivity. *First Monday*, 19 (8). Available at: http://dx.doi.org/10.5210/fm.v19i8.4902 (accessed March 1, 2018).

Nyberg, A. K. (1995). Comic Books and Women Readers: Trespassers in Masculine Territory. In P.C. Rollins & S. W. Rollins, *Gender in Popular Culture: Images of Men and Women in Literature, Visual Media, and Material Culture*. Cleveland, OH: Ridgemont Press, pp. 205–224.

(2016). The Comics Code. In F. Bramlett, R. T. Cook, & A. Meskin, eds., *The Routledge Companion to Comics*. London: Routledge, pp. 25–33.

(2002). Poisoning Children's Culture: Comics and Their Critics. In L. Cushman Schurman & D. Johnson, eds., *Scorned Literature: Essays*

References

    on the History and Criticism of Popular Mass-Produced Fiction in America. Westport, CT: Greenwood Press, pp. 167–186.

    (1998). *Seal of Approval: The History of the Comics Code*. Jackson, MS: University Press of Mississippi.

Orme, S. (2016). Femininity and Fandom: The Dual-Stigmatisation of Female Comic Book Fans, *Journal of Graphic Novels and Comics* 7 (4), 403–416.

Parsons, P. (1991). Batman and His Audience: The Dialectic of Culture. In R. E. Pearson & W. Uricchio, eds., *The Many Lives of the Batman: Critical Approaches to a Superhero and His Media*. New York, NY: Routledge; BFI Publishing, pp. 66–89.

Proctor, W. & Kies, B. (2018). Editors' Introduction: On Toxic Fan Practices and the New Culture Wars. *Participations* 15(1). Available at: www.participations.org/Volume%2015/Issue%201/8.pdf (ccessed October 15, 2018).

Pustz, M. (1999). *Comic Book Culture: Fanboys and True Believers*. Jackson, MI: University Press of Mississippi.

Rehberg Sedo, D. (2011). *Reading Communities from Salons to Cyberspace*. Houndmills, UK: Palgrave Macmillan.

Reisdorf, B. C., Axelsson, A., & Söderholm, H. M. (2012). Living Offline: A Qualitative Study of Internet Non-Use in Great Britain and Sweden. Paper presented at the 13th annual international and interdisciplinary conference of the Association of Internet Researchers (AoIR), Salford, UK, October 18–21. Available at: http://spir.aoir.org/index.php/spir/article/view/10 (accessed March 15, 2018).

Robbins, T. (1999). *Girls to Grrrlʒ: A History of [Women's] Comics from Teens to Zines*. San Francisco, CA: Chronicle Books.

    (2013). *Pretty in Ink: American Women Cartoonists, 1896–2013*. Seattle, WA: Fantagraphics.

Ross, C. S. (1999). Finding without Seeking: The Information Encounter in the Context of Reading for Pleasure. *Information Processing & Management*, 35 (6), 783–799.

(1995). If They Read Nancy Drew, so What? Series Book Readers Talk Back. *Library & Information Science Research*, 17 (3), 201–236.

(2001). Making Choices: What Readers Say about Choosing Books to Read for Pleasure. *Acquisitions Librarian*, 13 (25), 5–21.

(2009). Reader on Top: Public Libraries, Pleasure-Reading, and Models of Reading. *Library Trends*, 57 (4), 632–656.

Ross, C. S., McKechnie, L., & Rothbauer, P. M. (2006). *Reading Matters: What the Research Reveals about Reading, Libraries, and Community*. Westport, CT: Libraries Unlimited.

(2018). *Reading Still Matters: What the Research Reveals about Reading, Libraries, and Community*. Westport, CT: Libraries Unlimited.

Rothbauer, P. M. (2009). Exploring the Placelessness of Reading among Older Teens in a Canadian Rural Municipality. *Library Quarterly*, 79 (4), 465–483.

(2004). Finding and Creating Possibility: Reading in the Lives of Lesbian, Bisexual and Queer Young Women. PhD diss., University of Western Ontario.

(2011). Rural Teens on the Role of Reading in their Lives. *Journal of Research on Libraries and Young Adults*, 1 (2). Available at: www .yalsa.ala.org/jrlya/2011/02/rural-teens-on-the-role-of-reading-in-their-lives/ (accessed March 1, 2018).

Rothbauer, P., Skjerdingstad, K. I., McKechnie, L., and Oterholm, K. (eds.) (2016). *Plotting the Reading Experience: Theory, Practice, Politics*. Waterloo, ON: Wilfrid Laurier University Press.

Rouncefield, M. & Tolmie, P. (2011). Digital Words: Reading and the 21st Century Home. In R. Harper, ed., *The Connected Home:*

The Future of Domestic Life. London: Springer London, pp. 133–162.

Ruecker, S. (2002). Carrying the Pleasure of Electronic Books. In P. W. Jordan & W. S. Green, eds., *Pleasure with Products: Beyond Usability*. London: Taylor & Francis, pp. 135–145.

Sabeti, S. (2012b). "Arts of Time and Space": The Perspectives of a Teenage Audience on Reading Novels and Graphic Novels. *Participations*, 9 (2), 159–179. Available at: www.participations.org/Volume%209/Issue% 202/11%20Sabeti.pdf (accessed September 15, 2018).

(2013). A Different Kind of Reading: The Emergent Literacy Practices of a School-Based Graphic Novel Club. *British Educational Research Journal* 39 (5), 835–852.

(2011). The Irony of "Cool Club": The Place of Comic Book Reading in Schools. *Journal of Graphic Novels and Comics*, 2 (2), 137–149.

(2012a). Reading Graphic Novels in School: Texts, Contexts and the Interpretive Work of Critical Reading. *Pedagogy, Culture & Society*, 20 (2), 191–210.

Schenkel, K. (May 2015). On Female-Friendly Comic Shops. *BookRiot*. Available at: https://bookriot.com/2015/05/27/female-friendly-comic-shop-recommendations/ (accessed April 15, 2018).

Schenker, B. (August 2018b). Demo-Graphics: Comic Fandom on Facebook – European Edition. *Graphic Policy: Where Comic Books and Politics Meet* ... Available at: https://graphicpolicy.com/2018/08/17/demo-graphics-comic-fandom-facebook-european-edition-14/ (accessed October 15, 2018).

(October 2018a). Demo-Graphics: Comic Fandom on Facebook – US Edition. *Graphic Policy: Where Comic Books and Politics Meet* ... Available at: https://graphicpolicy.com/2018/10/16/demo-graphics-comic-fandom-facebook-us-edition-16-2/ (accessed October 15, 2018).

References

Schwarz, G. and Crenshaw, C., 2011. Old Media, New Media: The Graphic Novel As Bildungsroman. *Journal of Media Literacy Education*, 3 (1), 47–53.

Scott, S. (2013). Fangirls in Refrigerators: The Politics of (in) Visibility in Comic Book Culture. *Transformative Works and Cultures* (13), 1–22.

Selwyn, N. (2003). Apart from Technology: Understanding People's Non-Use of Information and Communication Technologies in Everyday Life. *Technology in Society*, 25 (1), 99–116.

(2006). Digital Division or Digital Decision? A Study of Non-Users and Low-Users of Computers. *Poetics*, 334 (4–5), 273–292.

Sena, J. (2012). The e-Books and e-Readers: Evolution, Diffusion and Acceptance. *International Journal of the Book*, 9 (1), 79–93.

Snowball, C. (2011). Graphic Novels: Enticing Teenagers into the Library. PhD diss., Curtin University of Technology.

(2007). Researching Graphic Novels and their Teenage Readers. *LIBRES*, 17 (1), 1–20. Available at: http://libres.curtin.edu.au/libres17n1/ (accessed March 1, 2018).

(2005). Teenage Reluctant Readers and Graphic Novels. *Young Adult Library Services*, 3 (4), 43–45.

(2008). Teenagers Talking about Reading and Libraries. *Australian Academic and Research Libraries*, 39 (2), 106–118.

Sousanis, N. (2015). *Unflattening*. Cambridge, MA: Harvard University Press.

Stein, D. & Thon, J. (2013). *From Comic Strips to Graphic Novels: Contributions to the Theory and History of Graphic Narrative*. Berlin; Boston, MA: De Gruyter.

Tilley, C. L. (2014). Comics: A Once-Missed Opportunity. *Journal of Research on Libraries and Young Adults*, 1–18. Available at: www.yalsa.ala.org/jrlya/2014/05/comics-a-once-missed-opportunity/ (accessed March 1, 2018).

(2007). Of Nightingales and Supermen: How Youth Services Librarians Responded to Comics between the Years 1938 and 1955. PhD diss., Indiana University.

References

(2012). Seducing the Innocent: Fredric Wertham and the Falsifications that Helped Condemn Comics. *Information & Culture*, 47 (4), 383–413.

Tinker, E. (2007). Manuscript in Print: The Materiality of Alternative Comics. *Literature Compass*, 4 (4), 1169–1182.

Turkle, S. (2007). Introduction. In S. Turkle, ed., *Evocative Objects: Things We Think With*. Cambridge, MA: MIT Press, pp. 3–10.

Tveit, Å. K. & Mangen, A. (2014). A Joker in the Class: Teenage Readers' Attitudes and Preferences to Reading on Different Devices. *Library & Information Science Research*, 36 (3–4), 179–184.

United Nations Educational, Scientific and Cultural Organization (UNESCO) (2017). What Do We Mean by "Youth"? Available at: www.unesco.org/ new/en/social-and-human-sciences/themes/youth/youth-definition/ (accessed April 15, 2018).

Van Manen, M. (1997). *Researching Lived Experience: Human Science for an Action Sensitive Pedagogy*. London, ON: Althouse Press.

Willis, I. (2018). *Reception*. London: Routledge.

Wolfe, K. & Fiske, M. (1949). The Children Talk about Comics. In P. Lazarsfeld & F. Stanton, eds., *Communications Research, 1948–1948*. New York, NY: Harper and Bros., pp. 3–50.

Woo, B. (2011). The Android's Dungeon: Comic-Bookstores, Cultural Spaces, and the Social Practices of Audiences. *Journal of Graphic Novels and Comics*, 2 (2), 125–136.

Wright, B. W. (2003). *Comic Book Nation: The Transformation of Youth Culture in America*. Baltimore, MD: Johns Hopkins University Press.

Ytre-Arne, B. (2011b). "I Want to Hold It in My Hands": Readers' Experiences of the Phenomenological Differences between Women's Magazines Online and in Print. *Media, Culture & Society*, 33 (3), 467–477.

References

(2011a). Women's Magazines and Their Readers: The Relationship between Textual Features and Practices of Reading. *European Journal of Cultural Studies*, 14 (2), 213–228.

Zorbaugh, H. (1944). The Comics – There They Stand! *Journal of Educational Sociology*, 18 (4), 196–203.

Primary Texts

Angel. (2000–2002). 2 vols. Milwaukie, OR: Dark Horse.

Brown, C. (2014). *I Never Liked You: A Comic-Strip Narrative*. Montreal: Drawn & Quarterly.

Buffy the Vampire Slayer Season Eight. (2007–2011). 8 vols. Milwaukie, OR: Dark Horse.

Busiek, K., Nicieza, F., & Bagley, M. (2009). *Trinity*. 2 vols. New York, NY: DC Comics.

Ennis, G. & Dillon, S. (1996–2001). Preacher. 9 vols. New York, NY: DC Comics.

Gaiman, N. (1991–1997). The Sandman. 10 vols. New York, NY: DC Comics.

Gaiman, N. & Russell, C. P. (2008). *Coraline*. New York, NY: HarperCollins.

Guibert, E., Lefèvre, D., & Lemercier, F. (2009). *The Photographer*. New York, NY: First Second.

Larcenet, M. (2005). *Ordinary Victories*. 2 vols. New York, NY: NBM.

Moore, A. & Lloyd, D. (1989). *V for Vendetta*. New York, NY: DC Comics.

Morrison, G. (1996–2001). The Invisibles. 7 vols. New York, NY: DC Comics.

O'Malley, B. L. (2004–2010). *Scott Pilgrim*. Portland, OR: Oni Press.

Ōtomo, K. (2000–2002). *Akira*. 6 vols. Milwaukie, OR: Dark Horse Comics.

Rabagliati, M. (2000–). Paul.Montreal: Drawn & Quarterly.

Satrapi, M. (2003–2004). Persepolis. New York, NY: Pantheon.

References

Schrag, A. (1997). *Awkward*. San Jose, CA: Slave Labor Graphics.

(1997). *Definition*. San Jose, CA: Slave Labor Graphics.

(2004). *Likewise*. San Jose, CA: Slave Labor Graphics.

(2000). *Potential*. San Jose, CA: Slave Labor Graphics.

Shanower, E., Young, S., & Baum, F. L. (2009). *The Wonderful Wizard of Oz*. New York, NY: Marvel.

Spiegelman, A. (1986–1991). *Maus: A Survivor's Tale*. 2 vols. New York, NY: Pantheon.

Thompson, C. (2003). *Blankets: A Graphic Novel*. Marietta, GA: Top Shelf.

Vaughan, B. K. & Guerra, P. (2003–2008). *Y: The Last Man*. 10 vols. New York, NY: DC Comics.

Ware, C. (1995). *Jimmy Corrigan, the Smartest Kid on Earth*. Seattle, WA: Fantagraphics Books.

Acknowledgments

I would like to recognize my participants; without you this work would not be here. I cannot be grateful enough for your time and for your sharing your passion, your thoughts, and your experiences with me. To Cath, Lynne, and Paulette for providing more than just an intellectual home. To my Canadian and Spanish families. To NKD.

Cambridge Elements

Publishing and Book Culture

Series Editor:
Samantha Rayner
University College London

Samantha Rayner is a Reader in UCL's Department of Information Studies. She is also Director of UCL's Centre for Publishing, co-Director of the BloomsburyCHAPTER(Communication History, Authorship, Publishing, Textual Editing and Reading) and co-editor of the Academic Book of the Future BOOC (Book as Open Online Content) with UCL Press.

Associate Editor:
Rebecca Lyons
University of Bristol

Rebecca Lyons is a Teaching Fellow at the University of Bristol. She is also co-editor of the experimental BOOC (Book as Open Online Content) at UCL Press. She teaches and researches book and reading history, particularly female owners and readers of Arthurian literature in fifteenth- and sixteenth-century England, and also has research interests in digital academic publishing.

Advisory Board:

Alexis Weedon, University of Bedfordshire

Alan Staton, Booksellers Association

Angus Phillips, Oxford International Centre for Publishing

Richard Fisher, Yale University Press

John Maxwell, Simon Fraser University

Shafquat Towheed, The Open University

Jen McCall, Emerald Publishing

ABOUT THE SERIES:

This series aims to fill the demand for easily accessible, quality texts available for teaching and research in the diverse and dynamic fields of Publishing and Book Culture. Rigorously researched and peer-reviewed Elements will be published under themes, or 'Gatherings'. These Elements should be the first check point for researchers or students working on that area of publishing and book trade history and practice: we hope that, situated so logically at Cambridge University Press, where academic publishing in the UK began, it will develop to create an unrivalled space where these histories and practices can be investigated and preserved.

Cambridge Elements

Publishing and Book Culture
Young Adult Publishing

Gathering Editor: Melanie Ramdarshan Bold
Melanie Ramdarshan Bold is Associate Professor at University College
London. Her main research interest centres on contemporary authorship,
publishing, and reading, with a focus on books for children and young
adults. She is the author of Inclusive Young Adult Fiction: Authors of
Colour in the United Kingdom (2018).

ELEMENTS IN THE GATHERING

A full series listing is available at: www.cambridge.org/EPBC

Printed in the United States
By Bookmasters